CW00419313

Apache JMeter

A practical beginner's guide to automated testing and performance measurement for your websites

Emily H. Halili

PUBLISHING

BIRMINGHAM - MUMBAI

Apache JMeter

Copyright © 2008 Packt Publishing

All rights reserved. No part of this book may be reproduced, stored in a retrieval system, or transmitted in any form or by any means, without the prior written permission of the publisher, except in the case of brief quotations embedded in critical articles or reviews.

Every effort has been made in the preparation of this book to ensure the accuracy of the information presented. However, the information contained in this book is sold without warranty, either express or implied. Neither the author, Packt Publishing, nor its dealers or distributors will be held liable for any damages caused or alleged to be caused directly or indirectly by this book.

Packt Publishing has endeavored to provide trademark information about all the companies and products mentioned in this book by the appropriate use of capitals. However, Packt Publishing cannot guarantee the accuracy of this information.

First published: June 2008

Production Reference: 1200608

Published by Packt Publishing Ltd.
32 Lincoln Road
Olton
Birmingham, B27 6PA, UK.

ISBN 978-1-847192-95-0

www.packtpub.com

Cover Image by Vinayak Chittar (vinayak.chittar@gmail.com)

Credits

Author

Emily H. Halili

Reviewer

Charitha.Kankanamgc

Acquisition Editor

Viraj Joshi

Development Editor

Ved Prakash Jha

Technical Editor

Darshana D.Shinde

Editorial Team Leader

Mithil Kulkarni

Project Manager

Abhijeet Deobhakta

Project Coordinator

Patricia Weir

Indexer

Rekha Nair

Proofreader

Chris Smith

Production Coordinators

Aparna Bhagat

Shantanu Zagade

Cover Work

Aparna Bhagat

About the Author

Emily H. Halili Since graduating in 1998, from California State University in Computer Science, Emily H. Halili has taken numerous roles in the IT/Software industry — namely as Software Engineer, Network Engineer, Lecturer, and Trainer. Currently a QA Engineer in CEO Consultancy-Malaysia with great passion for testing, she has two years of experience in software testing and managing QA activities. She is an experienced manual tester and has practical knowledge of various open-source automation tools and frameworks, including JMeter, Selenium, JProfiler, Badboy, Sahi, Watij, and many more.

My heartfelt thanks to my husband, Duraid Fatouhi, whom without his faith in me, this book may never see the light. To John VanZandt, president of CEO Consultancy, Malaysia – who inspires creativity and comradeship at work. To my colleagues at CEO Consultancy and ex-colleagues, for constantly challenging me with testing tasks and much more. Lastly, but the least, my daughter, Zahraa for inspiring.

Table of Contents

Preface

JMeter is a powerful, easy-to-use, and FREE load-testing tool. Those are my first impressions of JMeter, a testing tool I've recently fallen in love with—not blindly. With this book, I share with you my experience with JMeter.

When I was first assigned to use JMeter to perform testing on a particular web application, I went all out looking for anything on JMeter. Despite plenty of online manuals, article and newsgroup posts, printed or e-books were nowhere to be found. So, when one of the editors of Packtpub approached me with this idea of writing a book on JMeter, I could hear myself saying: "Had there been a book on JMeter, I would have bought one at any cost. Since no one has written any, why not I write one?" After much contemplation and work, here is the result—what you are reading right now.

What The Book Is About

This book is about using basic testing tools in JMeter that support software load and regression test automation. JMeter can be used to test static and dynamic resources over a wide range of client/server software (e.g. web applications). For simplicity, this book will focus on a narrowed aspect of JMeter while demonstrating practical tests on both static and dynamic resources of a web application. As this small book is an introductory reference, it is ideally designed to pave the path for the reader to get more detailed insight on JMeter, and what more it can do beyond this reference.

What This Book Covers

Chapter 1: Automated Testing

The reader who is already automating their tests may want to skip this chapter. It takes a quick look at the need to automate testing and whether automation suits all needs of testing. It provides a quick look at and evaluation of test automation.

Chapter 2: Introduction to JMeter

This chapter is an overview of JMeter, as it takes a glance at its young history, the general look-and-feel of its GUI design, requirements, and its features.

Chapter 3: Getting Started

This chapter serves as a guide to the first-time user on installing and customizing the system environment as they run JMeter for the first time. The installation process will match the purpose of this book. Hence it will skip the more complex setup of the environment. A more complex setup guide is available from the home site of JMeter.

Chapter 4: The Test Plan

This chapter sets out to prepare the reader with the basic knowledge of tools required to successfully create and run tests. It prepares the reader for the next two chapters.

Chapter 5: Load/Performance Testing of Website

This chapter demonstrates the use of the tools in JMeter that support Load or Performance Testing. The walkthroughs are facilitated by illustrations, giving a more descriptive guide to both new and seasoned testers.

Chapter 6: Functional Testing

This chapter demonstrates the use of the tools in JMeter that support Functional or Regression Testing. Little is known of JMeter being used to support this testing approach. As in Chapter 5, the walkthroughs are facilitated by illustrations, giving a more descriptive guide to both new and seasoned testers.

Chapter 7: Advanced Features

This chapter briefly describes other resources that can be tested by using JMeter, i.e. HTTP Server, Database Server, FTP Server, using Regular Expressions, and much more. The reader may want to explore more of JMeter, once he/she has a good understanding of the basics this book covers.

Chapter 8: JMeter and Beyond

This chapter discusses briefly on what more JMeter has and can do for its users. It tells the reader where to go in order to find more information about other elements of JMeter that this book does not have.

What You Need for This Book

JMeter is a 100% pure Java desktop application. Hence, you need to first download and then install the latest production release from the Jakarta official download website: (`http://jakarta.apache.org/site/downloads/index.html`). Download the binary code from the JMeter package available on this site.

Who This Book Is For

The ideal readers or users of this book would be the experienced or novice testers who have been testing manually and now would like to automate their tests. Those testers who are already automating their testing using other tools or testing software may also want to use this book as they look for alternatives. This book would also be a good point for test Managers/ Leaders to start doing research on the test automation tool that may best suit their testing needs and of course, their budget. One of the many beauties of JMeter, is that one does not need to have prior programming skills to use it, making JMeter one of the most popular open-source testing tools within the testing community.

Conventions

In this book, you will find a number of styles of text that distinguish between different kinds of information. Here are some examples of these styles, and an explanation of their meaning.

There are three styles for code. Code words in text are shown as follows: "You may also change the default file format to save to XML, by editing the `jmeter. properties` file"

A code block is shown as follows. When we wish to draw your attention to a particular part of a code block, the relevant lines or items will be made bold:

```
<td id="ID">${VOL_g1}</td>\s*<td id="Name">${VOL_g2}</td>\s*
<td id="Email"><a href="mailto:vol${VOL_g1}@acme-volsys.net">
  vol${VOL_g1}@acme-volsys.net</a></td>\s*
<td id="URL"><a href="www.acme-volsys.net/~vol${VOL_g1}">
  www.acme-volsys.net/~vol${VOL_g1}</a></td>\s*
<td id="Phone">9999999, ext: ${VOL_g1}</td>
```

Any command-line input and output is written as follows:

```
jmeter -H 129.198.1.1 -P 8000 -u someusername -a someuserpassword -N
localhost
```

New terms and **important words** are introduced in a bold-type font. Words that you see on the screen, in menus or dialog boxes for example, appear in our text like this: "Clicking the **Forever** checkbox causes the test to run repeatedly until stopped manually".

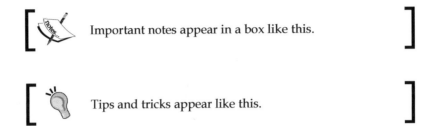

Important notes appear in a box like this.

Tips and tricks appear like this.

Reader Feedback

Feedback from our readers is always welcome. Let us know what you think about this book, what you liked or may have disliked. Reader feedback is important for us to develop titles that you really get the most out of.

To send us general feedback, simply drop an email to `feedback@packtpub.com`, making sure to mention the book title in the subject of your message.

If there is a book that you need and would like to see us publish, please send us a note in the **SUGGEST A TITLE** form on `www.packtpub.com` or email `suggest@packtpub.com`.

If there is a topic that you have expertise in and you are interested in either writing or contributing to a book, see our author guide on `www.packtpub.com/authors`.

Customer Support

Now that you are the proud owner of a Packt book, we have a number of things to help you to get the most from your purchase.

Downloading the Example Code for the Book

Visit `http://www.packtpub.com/files/code/2950_Code.zip` to directly downlad the example code.

The downloadable files contain instructions on how to use them.

Errata

Although we have taken every care to ensure the accuracy of our contents, mistakes do happen. If you find a mistake in one of our books—maybe a mistake in text or code—we would be grateful if you would report this to us. By doing this you can save other readers from frustration, and help to improve subsequent versions of this book. If you find any errata, report them by visiting `http://www.packtpub.com/support`, selecting your book, clicking on the **let us know** link, and entering the details of your errata. Once your errata are verified, your submission will be accepted and the errata will be added to the list of existing errata. The existing errata can be viewed by selecting your title from `http://www.packtpub.com/support`.

Questions

You can contact us at `questions@packtpub.com` if you are having a problem with some aspect of the book, and we will do our best to address it.

1
Automated Testing

Really, what is test automation? Is it something like pressing some button to turn on the testing on auto-pilot? To an extent, yes, you can have that, and more. According to Wikipedia, (`http://en.wikipedia.org/wiki/Test_automation`):

> *Test automation is the use of software to control the execution of tests, the comparison of actual outcomes to predicted outcomes, the setting up of test preconditions, and other test control, and test reporting functions.*

Simply put, it is the process of automating the manual testing process currently in use, by the use of software. Hence, this definition goes further than simply using some Word Processor software.

This chapter will give you a quick overview of what test automation is all about and its significance in the testing process, and ultimately, the software process. It aims to help you decide whether test automation is the way to go for testing applications. It will also describe the cost-effectiveness of test automation in comparison with manual testing or no testing at all.

As you begin to ponder if test automation is what you need, some questions may be lingering in your mind:

- Why do I need to automate software testing?
- How do I decide whether to automate or not?
- How much would test automation add to the total cost of testing?

This chapter will answer your questions.

Why Automate Testing?

Some software project managers hold strongly to the myth that testing costs too much, takes too much time, does not help them build the product, and can create hostility between the tester(s) and the development team. You will find these are the very people who would spend the least on testing.

On the other hand, there are smarter software managers who understand that testing is an investment in quality. Hence, they tend to spend more on testing. Efficient test project management produces a positive return, fits within the overall project schedule, has quantifiable findings, and is seen as a definite contributor to the project.

However, as developing software overruns, as it normally does, time is at a premium. As you may know or have experienced, 'manual' testing, especially regression testing can be exhausting. A time-consuming and tedious process, it is inefficient and conflicts with today's shorter application development cycles. As a result, it gets in the way to test an application thoroughly — enabling critical bugs to slip through undetected. What's more, manual tests are prone to human error and inconsistencies that can distort test results.

Can we do without automation? Yes, of course — if time is abundant and your client (or boss) is NOT on your tail for the application's next release. However, for most of the time, this is not the case. In software testing, time is a determining factor and the effective use of automation CAN help improve the testing speed.

On the other hand, despite of the appeals of test automation, we need to bear in mind that test automation may just be suitable for only parts of the software testing process. Automated testing IS NOT a total replacement for manual testing. Certain aspects of testing an application would rely more on the human tester than on test automation. The ultimate testers still are the human testers themselves; where applicable, test automation only complements manual testing. Test automation may not test any better than the human tester, but if implemented wisely, can certainly help the tester test faster. Since certain testing of the application can be automated, the tester can spend more quality time on more important and critical aspects of the testing. Ultimately, the tester can test better and more effectively.

To Automate or Not to Automate—Some Hints

The previous paragraph cautions against using automation to replace manual testing, putting you, the reader (or the tester) in an awkward predicament. However, let us think about an average-case scenario: You are pressed against a tight budget and schedule, and you are sure that manually regression testing the application completely would only leave you and your team physically and mentally exhausted. Would automation help you test, if not any better, at least faster? Some hints may just help you decide:

- Pick a good time to start automating:

  Automation is best used after the tester has grasped the fundamental testing skills and concepts through manual testing experience. Another good time is when the tests that are going to be repeated or simulated, as normally found in regression testing and performance testing, respectively. As this goes, not all testing approaches may justify the use of automation.

  Rex Black in his article, *Investing in Software Testing: Manual or Automated?* concludes that the decision to automate testing comes from the need to repeat tests numerous times or reduce the cycle time for test execution while *higher per-test costs and needs for human skills, judgment, and interaction incline towards decision to test manually.*

- Not *all* testing approaches are suitable to automate:

  Suitable: Acceptance, Compatibility, Load, Volume or Capacity, Performance and Reliability, Structural testing, Regression, Exception or Negative testing.

Type of Testing	Description (adapted from source: `http://www.istqb.org`)
Acceptance testing	Formal testing with respect to user needs, requirements, and business processes conducted to determine whether a system satisfies or does not satisfy the acceptance criteria and to enable the user, customers, or other authorized entity to determine whether or not to accept the system.
Compatibility testing	The process of testing to determine the interoperability of a software product.
Load testing	A type of performance testing conducted to evaluate the behavior of a component or system with increasing load, e.g. numbers of parallel users and/or numbers of transactions, to determine what load can be handled by the component or system.
Volume/Capacity testing	Testing where the system is subjected to large volumes of data.

Type of Testing	Description (adapted from source: http://www.istqb.org)
Performance testing	The process of testing to determine the performance of a software product.
Reliability testing	The process of testing to determine the reliability of a software product.
Structural testing	Testing based on an analysis of the internal structure of the component or system (also known as white-box testing)
Regression testing	Testing of a previously tested program following modification to ensure that defects have not been introduced or uncovered in unchanged areas of the software, as a result of the changes made.
Exception testing	Testing behavior of a component or system in response to erroneous input, from either a human user or from another component or system, or due to an internal failure.
Negative testing	Tests aimed at showing that a component or system does not work.

Not suitable: Installation and setup, Configuration and Compatibility, Documentation and help, Error handling and Recovery, Localization, Usability, and any other that relies heavily on human judgment.

Type of Testing	Description (adapted from source: http://www.istqb.org)
Installation and setup testing	Testing that focuses on what customers will need to do to install and set up the new software successfully.
Configuration testing	The process of testing the installability or configurability of a software product.
Compatibility testing	Testing to evaluate the application's compatibility with the computing environment.
Documentation testing	Testing the quality of the documentation, e.g. user guide or installation guide.
Error handling testing	Testing to determine the ability of applications system to properly process the incorrect transactions.
Recovery testing	Testing how well the software is able to recover from crashes, hardware failures, and other similar problems.
Localization testing	Testing that focuses on internationalization and localization aspects of software in adapting a globalized application to a particular culture/locale.
Usability testing	Testing to determine the extent to which the software product is understood, easy to learn, easy to operate, and attractive to the users under specified conditions.

A point worthy of note is that there are tests that may justify the use of both manual and automated testing. These include: functionality testing, user interface, date and time handling, and use cases (user scenarios).

- Make automation only a supplement to a testing project:

In many cases, when a test requires the human mind making better judgments, use of automation merely accommodates that, but is not its replacement. For example, performing usability testing on application with a user interface designed for visually impaired users, no automation test can be any better than the human tester making judgments about the appropriate page element sound, size, or colors that would benefit the application's targeted users. While testing other aspects of the application, load testing or performance testing, for example, can be automated.

- Do some comparison of Automated vs. Manual Testing:

Manual Testing	Automated Testing
Running (and re-running) tests manually can be very time consuming.	Cost-effective, if you have to repeat tests numerous times.
All required tests need to be rerun each time there is a new build—which eventually would become very mundane and tiresome. Also, would wear out the tester.	Allows you to run automation against code that frequently evolves in a timely manner. Most suited to test codes within Agile software development framework.
Manual tests would have to be run sequentially.	Automated tests can be run simultaneously on different machines.
Time-consuming and tedious if testing a large test matrix. Highly error-prone.	Aids in testing a large test matrix.
If the test case only runs twice a coding milestone, it should most likely be a manual test. Less cost than automating it.	It costs more to set up and configure a test automation framework and test cases.
Better suited if you are testing UIs.	Cannot automate visual information. More suited for non-UI tests
It allows the tester to perform more ad hoc (random testing), which increases the odds of finding real user bugs.	Automation test tools are software themselves, and there is no 'perfect' software. Bugs may also surface in these tools.
Tester can do testing without automation.	Only suitable for portions of the testing process.

How Much Does it Cost?

The total cost needs to consider the costs of numerous resources undertaking a testing project. These resources generally include:

- Person hours to test—time to set up and perform automation
- Testing environment—testing infrastructure or environment
- Testing software—testing technology/tools

As our main focus is on the cost of testing software, it can range from high as six to seven figures per license to as little as $0 (free of charge, normally in the form of freeware or open-source code). However, as testing software relies on the tester and the environment in which the tests are executed, the total cost counts for more.

Rex Black's article provides us with a hypothetical scenario summarizing the cost of testing—no testing, manual testing and automated testing. An undisputed fact that any software project manager is aware of: bugs found by the customers are much more expensive than if the same bugs are found during development. Depicting a hypothetical example, the table below indicates that automation gives the client higher return on investment (ROI) than manual testing, while no testing at all brings no benefit in the long haul. I have taken the liberty to extend Rex's table to include the ROI if using an open-source testing software such as JMeter, as you will find in the last column.

Testing Investment Options: ROI Analysis

(Adapted from: `http://www.compaid.com/caiinternet/ezine/cost_of_quality_1.pdf`)

	No Formal Testing	Manual Testing	Automated Testing (from Vendor)	Automated Testing (Open Source – FOC)
Testing				
Staff	0.00	60,000.00	60,000.00	60,000.00
Infrastructure	0.00	10,000.00	10,000.00	10,000.00
Tools	0.00	0.00	12,500.00	0.00
Total Investment	0.00	70,000.00	82,500.00	70,000.00
Development				
Must-Fix Bugs Found	250.00	250.00	250.00	250.00
FixCost (Internal Failure)	2,500.00	2,500.00	2,500.00	2,500.00

	No Formal Testing	Manual Testing	Automated Testing (from Vendor)	Automated Testing (Open Source – FOC)
Testing				
Must-Fix Bugs Found	0.00	350.00	500.00	500.00
FixCost (Internal Failure)	0.00	35,000.00	50,000.00	50,000.00
Customer Support				
Must-Fix Bugs Found	750.00	400.00	250.00	250.00
FixCost (External Failure)	750,000.00	400,000.00	250,000.00	250,000.00
Cost of Quality				
Conformance	$0.00	$70,000.00	$82,500.00	$70,000.00
Nonconformance	$752,500.00	$437,500.00	$302,500.00	$302,500.00
Total COQ	$752,500.00	$507,500.00	$385,000.00	$372,500.00
Revenue	$752,500.00	$752,500.00	$752,500.00	$752,500.00
Return on Investment	#N/A	350%	445%	543%

Consequently, an effective combination of automated and manual testing, in the long run, may result in potentially cost-effective and efficient testing as it helps to shorten return on investment (ROI) of a software project.

Summary

How effective test automation is to a testing project depends heavily on whether automation really is what the testing team needs. Given that a testing team is comfortable with the idea of automating their tests (or ideally, part of their tests), automation can work wonders. Used effectively at the right turns of a testing project, it:

- Saves time
- Saves money
- Saves pride (normally hurt when you simply could not honor the datelines)

The next chapter will begin your experience with a freely distributed, application that is one of the most widely used open-source testing applications on earth—JMeter. This application has been stable for many years and its design is scalable so that an advanced user is free to use its source code to make his or her own version for exclusive use. Since it is available as an open-source project, anyone can contribute to the project development. You can too contribute.

2
Introduction to JMeter

At this point, we are aware of test automation and its related issues. If you decide to have test automation as a part of your testing project, then it's time for you to choose which test automation software to use. There are numerous test automation tools or softwares available, and they may cost from zero to tens of thousands of dollars. Your choice will depend on the needs, available resources, budget of the testing project, and certainly, the project funding. If you are faced with testing project challenges like tight budget and schedule and want a quick and reliable test automation solution to your testing needs, you are reading the right book—JMeter may just be what you are looking for. Why JMeter? For certain, JMeter, at the very least, meets these test automation criteria:

1. Zero acquisition cost—simply download the binaries from the URL. (`http://jakarta.apache.org/site/downloads/downloads_jmeter.cgi`).

2. Low learning curve—a basic knowledge of HTML and/or regular expressions helps too.

3. Versatile—can be used to test more than just web applications.

4. Scalable—its modular design allows components to be merged to support large-scale testing. Testing may also be run by more than one machine.

5. Extensible—API is available for customization.

6. Good support—online user manual, user forums, web notes, this book, etc.

This chapter will let you have your first encounter with JMeter. It will introduce JMeter, its promising beginning, and will give you an overview of what it is capable of. In addition, it will let you see the common user interface aspects of JMeter, and other important components of JMeter to give you a closer 'look and feel' about this test automation tool.

The Humble Beginning

JMeter is a desktop application, designed to test and measure the performance and functional behavior of client/server applications, such as web applications or FTP applications. It is by far, one of the most widely used open-source, freely distributed testing application that the Net can offer. It is purely Java-based and is highly extensible through a provided **API (Application Programming Interface)**. JMeter works by acting as the "client side" of a "client/server" application. It measures response time and all other server resources such as CPU loads, memory usage, and resource usage. In this respect, JMeter can be used effectively for functional test automation. In addition, it has tools that support regression testing of similar types of applications. Although it was originally designed for testing web applications, it has been extended to support other test functions. It was first and still is being developed as one of the Apache Jakarta Projects (`http://jakarta.apache.org`), as this project offer a diverse set of open-source Java solutions.

JMeter was first developed by **Stefano Mazzocchi** of the Apache Software Foundation. He wrote it primarily to test the performance of Apache JServ,which was later replaced by the Apache Tomcat Project. JMeter has since been developed and has expanded to load-test FTP servers, database servers, and Java Servlets and objects. Today, it has been widely accepted as a performance testing tool for web applications. Various companies, including AOL, have used JMeter to load-test their websites and SharpMind of Germany has used JMeter for functional and regression testing its applications and its clients.

The Features—What JMeter Can Do for You

JMeter may be used to test performance on static and dynamic resources such as static files, Servlets, FTP servers, Java Objects, Databases, Perl/CGI scripts, Queries, and more. In order to test and measure the robustness of an HTTP or FTP server or, network, testers need to provide simulation of multiple and different types of loads on these system objects. JMeter can help them do exactly that, and on a greater scale, too. Besides that, its graphical tools allow you to make better analysis of performance under heavy loads.

If you need to further test the functional behavior of your applications, there are tools in JMeter that can help you perform regression tests on your applications. Simply, its assertion tools, in addition to the test scripts, help to ensure whether your application is returning the expected results or not. Scalability and flexibility are also inherent in this aspect, as you can extend the assertions using regular expressions.

JMeter provides a user interface, making it more usable. It also exposes an API (Application Programming Interface) that allows you to run JMeter-based tests from a Java application.

The following excerpt is adapted from the Apache JMeter official website: `http://jakarta.apache.org/jmeter`. In detail, Apache JMeter features include:

- Performance testing of HTTP and FTP servers, and database queries
- 100% Java-based, hence has features that any Java application has:
  - Portability: can run on any JVMs
  - Concurrency: by many threads and of different functions by separate thread groups
  - Extensible:
    - Unlimited testing capabilities—various samplers can be used
    - Pluggable timers allow simulation of various types of loads
    - API and/or plug-ins allow great extendibility as well as customization
    - Built-in functions can be used to provide dynamic input to a test
    - Scriptable Samplers
- Efficient GUI (Java Swing) design and lightweight component support allows faster execution and more accurate timings
- Caching of test results and data providing offline analysis/replaying of test results

The most basic JMeter test script or test plan may involve creating a loop that simulates sequential requests to the server with a pre-defined interval and a thread group that simulates a concurrent load. The scripts can be customized and extended, providing you with the necessary tools that allow you to test and measure the performance and behavior of your application and/or server. Meanwhile, the basic elements of a JMeter test plan may include at least these three elements: Thread Group, Listeners, and Samplers. The Thread Group element simulates a group of users, which contains at least one user. As a Sampler element makes requests to the target server, a Listener element captures the response data or page following each request. Chapter 4 will explain the functions of these elements in detail.

The Look-How-Easy-to-Use GUI

A typical test plan will consist of one or more Thread Groups, logic controllers, listeners, timers, assertions, and configuration elements:

- Thread Group—each thread simulates a single user. All elements of a test plan must be under a thread group.

- Listeners—Provide access to the information gathered by JMeter about the test cases while JMeter runs.

- Controllers—Samplers tell JMeter to send requests to a server, while Logical Controllers let you customize its logic.

- Timers—Allow JMeter to delay between each request that a thread makes.

- Assertions—Allow you to "test" that your application is returning the results you expect it to.

- Configuration Elements—Working closely with a Sampler, these can add to or modify requests.

The following screenshot lets you see the icons representing these elements:

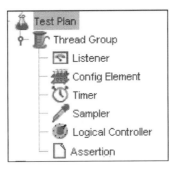

The user interface has two panels. Once JMeter runs, you will see two elements, **Test Plan** and **WorkBench**, as you see in the figure below. A Test Plan describes a series of steps JMeter will execute once the Test Plan runs, while a WorkBench functions as a temporary workspace to store test elements. Elements in the WorkBench are not saved with the Test Plan, but can be saved independently.

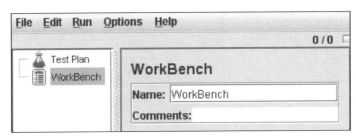

The left panel displays the elements/nodes used in our testing. Adding and Removing the elements are as easy as right-clicking a node and selecting **Add/Remove** respectively from the sub-menu. The right panel displays the details of each element.

The next sample you will see is a **Test Plan** consisting of more than one **Thread Group** and multiple elements in each Thread Group.

The following is a sample **Test Plan** having a single **Thread Group** incorporating multiple elements.

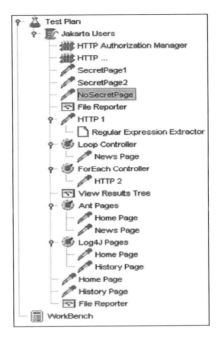

While using JMeter as a performance test tool, an essential element is the Thread Group. This element can be manipulated to simulate multiple data loads to test the server's behavior under stress loads. You can even preset a schedule by which the test can run. A sample **Thread Group** with details is shown below.

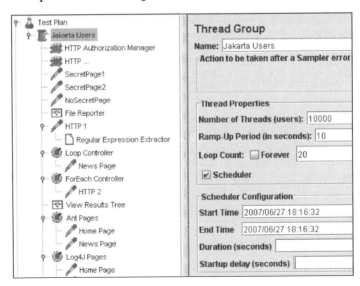

On the other hand, the same **Test Plan** can be extended to include functional/regression test properties by including Assertion elements as sub-elements as indicated by the following figures. The **Response Assertion** element shown in the following figure predefines the pattern matching conditions

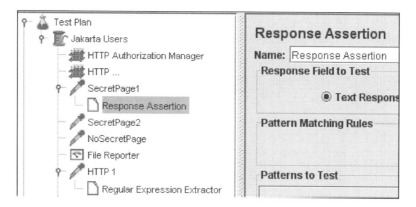

The **Assertion Results** element shown in following figure will capture these predefined patterns in the data or page response and display them for further analysis.

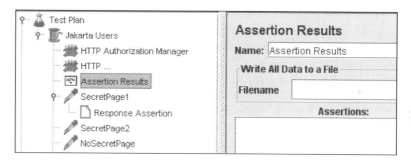

The Requirements

To be able to run JMeter, you will need at least **JVM (Java Virtual Machine) 1.3** as part your computing environment. If the application you are testing requires HTTPS protocol support, then you will need to download JSSE, since 1.3 does not provide that support. Also, it does not perform as well as later Java versions. Version 1.4 or higher is the ideal JVM to run JMeter at its best.

Since JMeter is Java-based, it can run on any system that has a Java implementation—making it highly portable. As far as operating system is concerned, JMeter has been able to run on UNIX, Linux, Open VMS Alpha 7.3+, and Windows (98 or higher)—in fact on any platform that has a JVM running on it.

If you plan to recompile the JMeter source code, as you extend JMeter using the API provided in the JMeter release, you may need to use the Java compiler via some IDE, e.g. Eclipse or any other Java IDE. You may also opt to use Ant to build JMeter from source. However, there is no need for you to install a separate Java compiler, as the JMeter distribution package would have a precompiled Java binary archive included. On the other hand, to build JMeter plug-ins or add-ons, there's no need to compile these JMeter classes. Simply download the binary archive and add the JARs to the JMeter classpath.

Also, you will need to download **JMeter stable version 1.8** or higher from the JMeter Apache website. You may choose either the Binary package (ready to use) or the Source package (if you plan to extend JMeter's functionality and build your own JMeter plug-ins).

There are other optional requirements if you want to use the more advanced features of JMeter. You can find out more on these options from the User's Manual. As this book will remain focused on JMeter on the Introductory level, I will leave you to explore on your own the more advanced features and requirements.

Summary

JMeter being a highly robust, scalable, and portable application makes it a suitable testing tool for today's non-proprietary, fast-changing, and market-driven application development process. Anyone with software testing experience or knowledge at any level will find JMeter easy to learn and use. One doesn't need programming expertise to realize the potential use of JMeter, but having it surely helps.

Despite the cliché that often trumpets open-source application as receiving little or no support, JMeter has abundant resources on the Web and newsgroups that may become your guiding light towards using JMeter most effectively. However, these third-party resources may give a fragmented approach to learn about JMeter, as I found most of them reiterate only narrowed aspects of JMeter. On the other hand, the JMeter distribution package provides a neat and detailed user manual, although some of the non-techie testers may find it quite technically intimidating. The same manual is available on JMeter's Apache official website. Once you are comfortable with it, I recommend that you experiment on your own (or you can refer to others' experiences) with the more advanced and technically-driven features of JMeter. However, as this book serves as a Beginner's guide to JMeter, this chapter and the rest of the chapters should become your first one-stop-reference or manual as you get familiar with using JMeter.

3
Getting Started

Chapter 2 got you acquainted with JMeter; this chapter will quickly lead you to start using it. While reading this chapter, you can simultaneously start using JMeter. All that you need before you start is an Internet-ready PC or notebook with JVM already installed and a live Internet connection. Further and more detailed requirements have been mentioned in the last chapter.

This chapter will provide you with a step-by-step guide and information on how to proceed with JMeter. At the end of this chapter, you will have already downloaded, installed, set up, and run JMeter, and be ready to start writing your first Test Plan.

Installing JMeter

You need to first download and then later install the latest production release from the Jakarta official download website: (http://jakarta.apache.org/site/downloads/index.html). Once downloaded, simply unzip the file into your favorite installation path. No further installation process is necessary.

 However, if you plan to perform remote testing using JMeter, avoid installing into a path whose name contains a space as this will not allow remote testing to work. This is currently a shortcoming of JMeter's remote testing.

You may also download the nightly build: (http://jakarta.apache.org/builds/jakarta-jmeter/nightly), but I would recommend this only if you are comfortable working with a beta-quality application. The installation of the nightly build version is just as easy as installing the latest production release.

Setting the Environment

The entire environment required to run JMeter is to have JVM running in your machine. You can download JSSE 1.3 or higher (1.4 or higher is the best) from Sun's official website: (http://java.sun.com/javase/downloads). Follow the instructions on the website so you can download the JVM needed to run JMeter. The site will also indicate to you how to set the JAVA_HOME environment variable.

Once the JVM is set and running and the JMeter release or nightly build is unzipped into the path of your choice, you are ready to run JMeter.

Running JMeter

Simply look for the bin directory in your JMeter installation path. On Windows systems, run jmeter.bat. If you are running JMeter under a UNIX environment, you will need to run the file jmeter.

In this process, JMeter automatically finds classes from JARs in its lib and lib/ext directories. Therefore, if in the future you have developed new JMeter components, you will need to jar them, and copy them into JMeter's lib/ext directory. You can also install utility JAR files in $JAVA_HOME/jre/lib/ext.

On a different note, if you are running JMeter from behind a firewall/proxy, you will need to provide JMeter with the server hostname and port number. Simply run the jmeter.bat/jmeter file from a command line along with these parameters:

- **-H** [proxy server hostname or ip address] OR **--proxyHost** [proxy server hostname or IP address

- **-P** [proxy server port] OR --proxyPort [proxy server port]

- **-N** [nonproxy hosts] (e.g. * .apache.org | localhost)

- **-u** [username for proxy authentication — if required] OR **--username** [username for proxy authentication — if required]

- **-a** [password for proxy authentication — if required] OR **--password** [password for proxy authentication — if required]

Example:

```
jmeter -H 129.198.1.1 -P 8000 -u someusername -a someuserpassword -N
localhost
```

Alternatively, if you choose to run JMeter without the GUI, you may use the following parameters as you run JMeter from command line:

-n This specifies JMeter is to run in non-GUI mode.

-t [name of JMX file that contains the Test Plan]

-l [name of JTL file to log sample results to]

-r Run all remote servers specified in jmeter.properties.

-H [proxy server hostname or IP address, if run via firewall/proxy]

-P [proxy server port, if run via firewall/proxy]

Example:

```
jmeter -n -t test1.jmx -l logtest1.jtl -H 198.162.1.1 -P 8000
```

 You can refer to the following website: http://jakarta.apache.
org/jmeter/usermanual/get-started.html.

You may also run JMeter in server mode in supporting distributed testing, designed to increase load on a server, but we will skip this part until you are ready to be an advanced JMeter user, taking into consideration the purpose of this book. If you are already curious, you can look at the online manual on Remote Testing: (http://jakarta.apache.org/jmeter/usermanual/remote-test.html).

Summary

This chapter is relatively simple to understand and follow, provided that you already have JVM (1.3 or higher) installed. Installing and running JMeter is a snap. Click on jmeter.bat (or jmeter on UNIX) and you are ready to start writing your first Test Plan. The following chapter will directly introduce you to the heartbeat of JMeter: the **Test Plan**.

4
The Test Plan

Installing and running JMeter is incredibly easy, as you have seen in Chapter 3. This chapter will be a reality check—meaning the Test Plan is what JMeter is all about. If you have written or have used a test script/case before, you are ready to write a JMeter Test Plan. In a simple analogy, JMeter Test Plan encapsulates a test script that you would have written manually otherwise. This chapter will lead you further into knowledge of JMeter's individual components that build up a Test Plan for the purpose of our Test Plan walkthroughs later. This chapter aims to equip you with knowledge of JMeter Test Plan and its related components, so you can be more prepared to write a JMeter Web Test Plan for the purpose of this book.

What Is a Test Plan?

A Test Plan defines and provides a layout of how and what to test: the web application as well as the client server application. It can be viewed as a container for running tests. It provides a framework in which it will execute a sequence of operations or tools to perform the testing. A test plan includes elements such as thread groups, logic controllers, sample-generating controllers, listeners, timers, assertions, and configuration elements. A test plan must have at least one thread group.

The simplest Test Plan normally includes the following elements:

- **Thread group**—These elements are used to specify number of running threads, a ramp-up period, and loop-count (no. of times to execute the test). Each thread simulates a user and the ramp-up period specifies the time to create all the threads. For example with 5 threads and 10 seconds of ramp-up time, it will take 2 seconds between each thread creation. The loop count defines the number of times the test will repeat for the thread group. The scheduler also allows you to set the start and end of the run time.

- **Samplers**—These configurable elements are used to send HTTP, FTP, SOAP/XML, JDBC, or LDAP requests to a server.

- **Listeners**—These elements are used to post-process request data. For example, you can save data to a file or illustrate the results with a chart. At this moment the JMeter chart does not provide many configuration options; however it is extensible and it is always possible to add an extra visualization or data processing module.

As you run JMeter, **Test Plan** will appear as default component along with **Workbench** on the left pane of the window.

The **Test Plan Control Panel** looks like this:

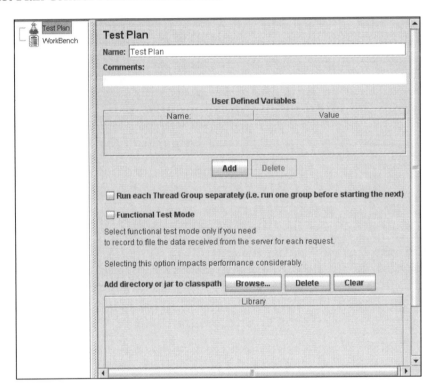

Each feature of this component is described as follows:

User Defined Variables: Here you can define static variables that allow you to extract repeated values throughout your tests, such as server names, port number, etc. For example, if you are testing an application on server `www.example-jmeter.net`, then you can define a variable called "server" with the value of `www.example-jmeter.net`. This value will replace variable "${server}" found anywhere in the test plan.

Option Functional Test Mode: This will cause JMeter to record the data returned from the server for each sample and write this data to the file that you have selected in your Listener. You may use the **Configuration** button on a listener to decide what fields to save. This can be useful if you are doing a small run to ensure that your server is returning the expected results. However, as this option allows JMeter to save the maximum sample information, JMeter's performance will reduce.

 If you are doing stress-testing, do not select this option, as it will affect your results.

If checked, this feature will save all information, including the full response log data and the default items, which are: time stamp, the data type, the label, the thread name, the response time, message, code, and a success indicator.

Option Run each Thread Group separately: If you have two or more Thread Groups in your Test Plan, selecting this will instruct JMeter to run each serially. Otherwise, JMeter will run Thread Groups simultaneously or in parallel.

Add directory or jar to classpath: This additive feature allows you to add JAR files or directories in case you have created your own extension to the JMeter package you are using. However, you will need to restart JMeter if you remove any entry.

Alternatively, you can copy all the jar files to the **jmeter | lib** directory. Another way to include additional libraries is to edit the JMeter properties file. In the `jmeter.properties` file, look for the entry "`#user.classpath=../classes;../jars/jar1.jar`. Edit this to include additional libraries. Avoid naming paths containing spaces as this may cause problems for Java.

Elements of a Test Plan

Elements or components of a JMeter Test Plan would comprise at least one Thread Group. Within each Thread Group we may place a combination of one or more of other elements: Sampler, Logic Controller, Configuration Element, Listener, and Timer. Each Sampler can be preceded by one or more Pre-processor element, followed by Post-processor element, and/or Assertion element. Let us look into each element in more detail.

Thread Group

A Thread Group is the starting point of a Test Plan, and it should contain all other JMeter elements. A thread group controls the threads that will be created by JMeter to simulate simultaneous users.

A Thread Group represents a group of users that will execute a particular test case. In its Control Panel, shown in the following figure, you will be able to simulate the "number of users", how long it takes to start each "user" (or how often the users should send requests), the number of times to perform the test (or how many requests they should send), and a start and stop time for each test.

Elements must be placed under a Thread Group as they define a Test Plan. A Thread Group controls the number of threads (or "users") JMeter will use to execute your test. If there are two or more Thread Groups in the same Test Plan, each Thread Group will execute completely independently from each other. Multiple Thread Groups within the same Test Plan simply simulate groups of concurrent, individual connections to your server application. The Control Panel allows us to configure each Thread Group to have its own set of specific "behaviors".

The **Thread Group Control Panel** looks like this:

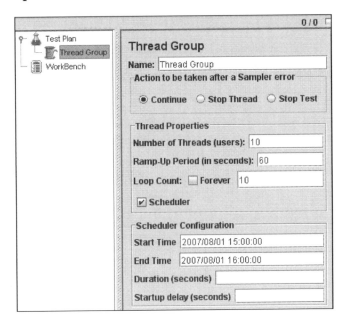

Each feature of this component is described as follows:

Action to be taken after a Sampler error: In case of any error recorded in any Sample as the test runs, you may let the test either: **Continue** to the next element in the test, or **Stop Thread** to stop the current Thread, or **Stop Test** completely, in case you want to inspect the error before continue running.

Number of Threads: Simulates the number of user(s) or connection(s) to your server application.

Ramp-Up Period: Defines how long it will take JMeter to get all threads running. For example, if there are 10 threads and a ramp-up period of 60 seconds, then each successive thread will be delayed by 6 seconds. In 60 seconds, all threads would be up and running. The best policy is to make your ramp-up period long enough to avoid large workload as the test begins, but short enough to allow the last one to start running before finishing the first one. You may set your ramp-up period to be equal with the number of threads, and later adjust accordingly.

Loop Count: Defines the number of times to execute the test. By default, the test is executed once but you can adjust as needed. Clicking the **Forever** checkbox causes the test to run repeatedly until stopped manually.

Scheduler checkbox: Once selected, the Scheduler Configuration section will appear at the bottom of the control panel.

Scheduler Configuration: Version 1.9 and later reveals this feature, where you can set the start and end time of running the test. Once you start the test, it will not execute any elements until the start time is reached. After each execution cycle, unless the end-time is reached, in which case the run is stopped, the iteration will continue until the **loop count** limit. The **startup delay** field allows JMeter some time before a thread is started and the **duration** field lets you define the duration of the whole test. The former overrides **start-time**, while the latter overrides **end-time**.

Controllers

JMeter has two types of Controllers:

1. **Samplers:**

   These allow JMeter to send specific types of requests to a server. In our sample tests later, we will be sending HTTP Requests the most, so we will use HTTP Request Sampler to let JMeter send those requests. You may add Configuration Elements to these Samplers to customize your server requests.

2. **Logic Controllers:**

   These allow you to customize the logic that JMeter uses to decide when to send requests. For example, you can use Random Controllers to send HTTP requests to the server randomly.

Samplers

JMeter Samplers allow you to define the requests that can be sent to a server. They simulate a user's request for a page from the target server. Each Sampler generates sample results that may have various attributes, such as performance, elapsed time, throughput, etc. By default, JMeter sends the requests in the order that the Samplers appear in the Test Plan tree. However, the order of processing the Samplers can be further customized using Logic Controllers. This will be further explained in the following section on "Logic Controllers".

You can customize each sampler by setting its properties, or you can add Configuration Elements. For the purpose of this book, since we will be sending numerous HTTP Requests to the same server, we may use the Default Configuration Element, which predefines the server to which all HTTP requests will be made.

An **HTTP Request Sampler Control Panel** looks like the following figure:

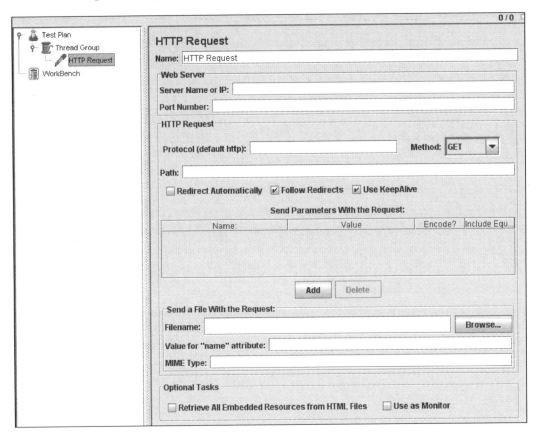

If you want JMeter to perform validation, you may add **Assertion** elements. More information on Assertion elements is available in a later section of this chapter.

A **Response Assertion** in an HTTP Request Sampler Control Panel looks like this:

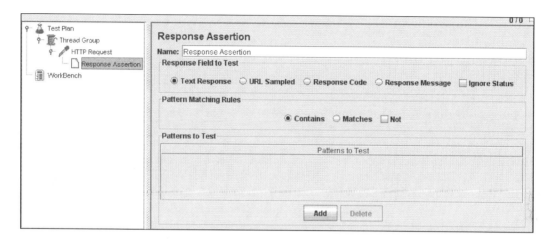

The following is a list of all Samplers JMeter provides:

- HTTP Request
- FTP Request
- JDBC Request
- Java Request
- SOAP/XML-RPC Request
- WebService (SOAP) Request
- LDAP Request
- LDAP Extended Request
- Access Log Sampler
- BeanShell Sampler
- BSF Sampler
- TCP Sampler
- JMS Publisher
- JMS Subscriber
- JMS Point-to-Point
- JUnit Request
- Mail Reader Sampler
- Test Action

Logic Controllers

Logic Controllers let you define the order of processing Samplers in a Thread, as you customize the logic that JMeter uses to send requests. A Logic Controller changes the order of requests that come from its sub-elements, or child elements. The child elements of a Logic Controller may comprise Samplers, Configuration Elements, and more Logic Controllers. For these requests, JMeter may randomly select (using Random Controller), repeat (using Loop Controller), interchange (using Interleave Controller) etc.

Several Logic Controllers can be combined to achieve various results.

A **Loop Controller Control Panel** looks like the following figure:

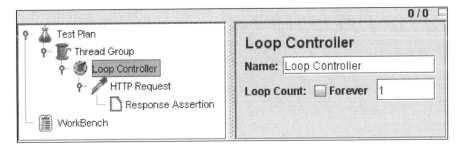

The following list consists of all the Logic Controllers JMeter provides:

- Simple Controller
- Loop Controller
- Once Only Controller
- Interleave Controller
- Random Controller
- Random Order Controller
- Throughput Controller
- Runtime Controller
- If Controller
- While Controller
- Switch Controller
- ForEach Controller
- Module Controller
- Include Controller
- Transaction Controller
- Recording Controller

Listeners

Listeners let you view the results of the Samplers in the form of tables, graphs, trees or simple text in some log files. They provide visual access to the data gathered by JMeter about the test cases as a Sampler component of JMeter is executed.

 Listeners collect data ONLY from elements at or below their level.

Each Listener displays the response information in specific way. For example, in order to view the graph form of the statistical data of the response time, you may want to use a "Aggregate Graph" Listener. Likewise, to view the statistical report on the same response data in a table form, you may want to add a "Summary Report" or "Aggregate Report" Listener. You can choose the form in which you would like to view the requests by selecting any of these Listeners, but they all write the same raw data to the output file with a .jtl extension.

 Listeners provide means to view, save, and read saved test results.

All Listeners that save data into the same file shows the same data differently.

As an example, the **Aggregate Graph Listener Control Panel** looks like the following figure:

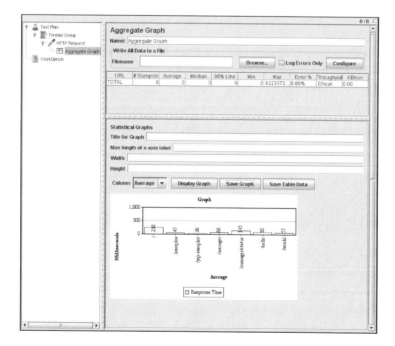

Some features common to all Listeners are:

Configure button: Use the "Configure" button to choose the information to write to the file for later use, or whether to save (with .jtl extension) in XML or CSV format—the latter being smaller and less detailed. This button is found in each Listener added to the Test Plan tree.

Once selected, the **Save Configuration** Window will appear as shown:

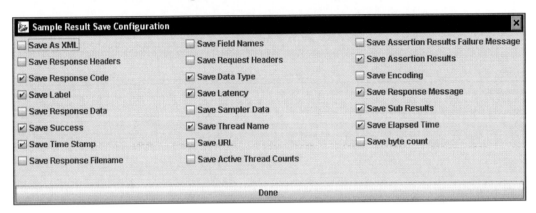

Browser button: Select this if you want to read and display a previously saved result.

 A Listener can use a lot of memory if there are a lot of Samples for which it is recording data.

 Jmeter will slow down if you have many listeners active. Therefore, use a minimum set of the most appropriate listeners.

One way to use the least memory possible is to save in the default CSV format and to use Simple Data Writer Listener.

You may also change the default file format to save to XML, by editing the jmeter.properties file. Look for this entry: jmeter.save.saveservice.output_ format=csv and simply change csv to xml if you opt for more detailed information.

The following list consists of all the Listeners JMeter provides:

- Sample Result Save Configuration
- Graph Full Results
- Graph Results
- Spline Visualizer
- Assertion Results
- View Results Tree
- Aggregate Report
- View Results in Table
- Simple Data Writer
- Monitor Results
- Distribution Graph (alpha)
- Aggregate Graph
- Mailer Visualizer
- BeanShell Listener
- Summary Report

Timers

A Timer Component is an option in building a Test Plan. It causes JMeter to pause for a certain amount of time between two successive requests that a Thread Group makes. As JMeter, by default, sends one request immediately after the other, which could overwhelm the server, adding a Timer will reduce the risk of breaking down the server's performance. This is especially useful if you are testing the application from its functional aspect.

However, you need to take care not to add too many Timers to a Thread Group, as JMeter will pause between two requests for the sum of all timers found in a Thread Group.

As an example, the **Constant Timer Control Panel** looks like this:

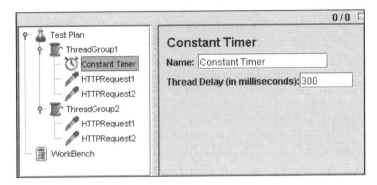

The following list consists of all the Timers JMeter provides:

- Constant Timer
- Gaussian Random Timer
- Uniform Random Timer
- Constant Throughput Timer
- Synchronizing Timer
- BeanShell Time

Assertions

Assertions allow you to include some validation test on the response of your request made using a Sampler. They are inserted as a child component of a Sampler. Assertions are particularly necessary in functional testing of your applications, while, in performance testing, you may want to use assertion to ensure the responses you receive. Do not contain content errors or missing sections, as this may affect the validity of your test.

[You can create these assertions using regular expressions.]

With Assertion, you can assert whether the application is returning the expected result or not. JMeter allows you to specify your assertions using Perl-style regular expressions.

Let's say, you want to ensure that, in an HTTP Request Sampler, the page you request contains the text 'Login Successful' to indicate successful access to a page. You may use **Response Assertion** to specify if the response does contain the text at all. If JMeter cannot find the text, then it will indicate this as failed request.

As an example, the **Response Assertion Control Panel** looks like this:

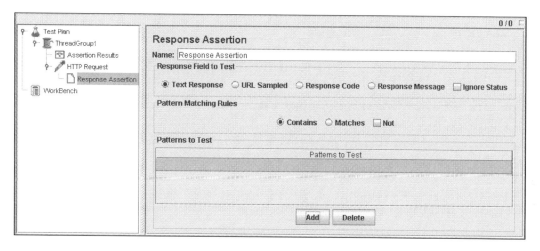

Associated with Assertions are Listeners such as "Assertion", "View Result in Table", "View Result Tree", "Aggregate Report" Listener, and "Summary Report" Listeners. Assertion results will be shown in detail in the first three Listeners, while the rest will show the failed assertions only as summary percentage of failure.

As an example, the Assertion Results Control Panel looks like the following figure:

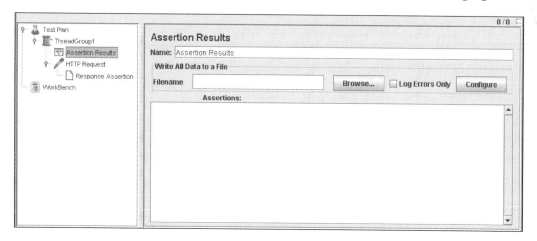

The following list consists of all the Assertions JMeter provides:

- Response Assertion
- Duration Assertion
- Size Assertion
- XML Assertion
- BeanShell Assertion
- MD5Hex Assertion
- HTML Assertion
- XPath Assertion
- XML Schema Assertion

Configuration Elements

Configuration Elements allow you to create defaults and variables to be used by Samplers. They are used to add or modify requests made by Samplers.

They are executed at the start of the scope of which they are part, before any Samplers that are located in the same scope. Therefore, a Configuration Element is accessed only from inside the branch where it is placed.

As an example, the **HTTP Request Defaults Control Panel** looks like this:

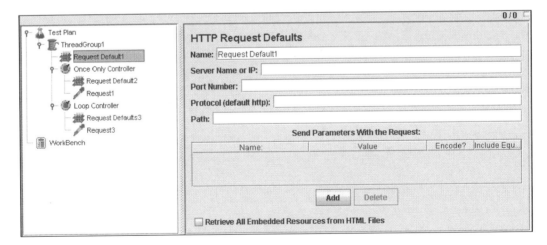

Request Default 1 is accessible to **Request1** and **Request3** Sampler, since it is in the 'Parent' branch of the Group, while **Request Default2** accessible only to **Request1** and **Request Default3** only to **Request3**, respectively.

The following list consists of all the Configuration Elements JMeter provides:

- CSV Data Set Config
- FTP Request Defaults
- HTTP Authorization Manager
- HTTP Cookie Manager
- HTTP Proxy Server
- HTTP Request Defaults
- HTTP Header Manager
- Java Request Defaults
- JDBC Connection Configuration
- Login Config Element
- LDAP Request Defaults
- LDAP Extended Request Defaults
- TCP Sampler Config
- User Defined Variables
- Simple Config Element

Pre-Processor Elements

Pre-processors allow you to modify the Samplers in their scope. They are often used to modify the settings of a Sample Request just before it runs, or to update variables that are not extracted from response text.

The following list consists of all the Pre-Processor Elements JMeter provides:

- HTML Link Parser
- HTTP URL Re-writing Modifier
- HTML Parameter Mask
- HTTP User Parameter Modifier
- User Parameters
- Counter
- BeanShell PreProcessor

Post-Processor Elements

Post-processors execute after a request has been made from a Sampler. A good way is to place them as a child of a Sampler, to ensure that it runs only after a particular Sampler, not to Sampler afterwards. This element is most often used to process the response data, for example, to retrieve particular value for later use.

The following list consists of all the Post-Processor Elements JMeter provides:

- Regular Expression Extractor
- XPath Extractor
- Result Status Action Handler
- Save Responses to a file
- Generate Summary Results
- BeanShell PostProcessor

Building a Test Plan That Tests Web Sites

This section will describe in brief how a basic Web Test Plan can be created. We will later expand this basic Test Plan to allow us to perform Performance Testing (Chapter 5) and Functional Testing (Chapter 6).

The elements that we will need for this basic Test Plan are as follows:

- Thread Group
- HTTP Request (Sampler)
- HTTP Request Default (Configuration Element)
- Summary Report (Listener)

Things to be done by us are as follows:

- Add Users
- Add and Configure Default HTTP Request
- Add HTTP Requests
- Add Listener to View/Store the Test Results
- Save & Run Test Plan

First of all, run JMeter (double-click `JMeter.bat` from `jmeter/bin`). You will see the default Elements, which are Test Plan and Workbench.

Adding Users

1. Simply right-click on the **Test Plan** icon on the left panel and select **Add | Thread Group**.

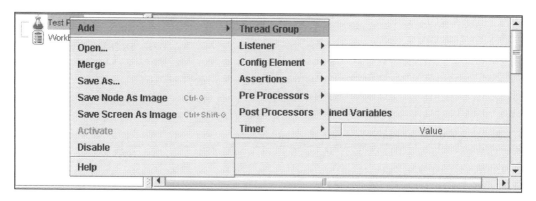

The right panel will display the Control Panel for the **Thread Group** you just added. We will not use the scheduler for this purpose.

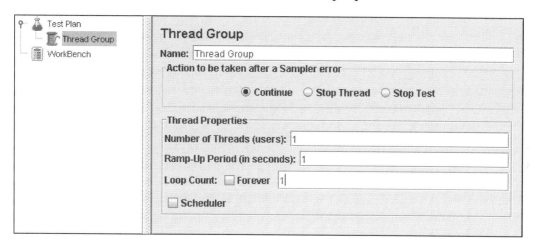

2. Rename the Thread Group using a more suitable name. Let's name this Group **My Users**.

3. For now, we will simulate the default: one-time connection and having one user (or connection/thread).

4. Change the **Ramp-Up Period** to **0**, meaning the User will start running immediately. If you have more than one user, having Ramp-Up Period 0 will cause all users to start running immediately and simultaneously.

The following figure displays how your JMeter should now look:

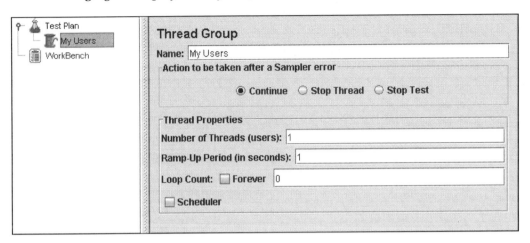

We are now ready to include more elements that define the tasks our "user" will perform.

- **Add Default HTTP Request**
    1. Right-click the **My Users** element to get the **Add menu**, and select **Add | Config Element | HTTP Request Defaults**.
    2. Select this new element to view its Control Panel.
    3. Rename the Element to **My URL**.
    4. In the **Server Name or IP** field, enter a URL: www.mocksite.net (or any other URL that you like to use). We will leave all other values as they are. Setting the HTTP Request Default Element will cause all other Request Sampler within this **My Users** to access to the same server. However, it does not make requests—it simply sets the request default for this Thread.

The following figure displays how your JMeter should now look:

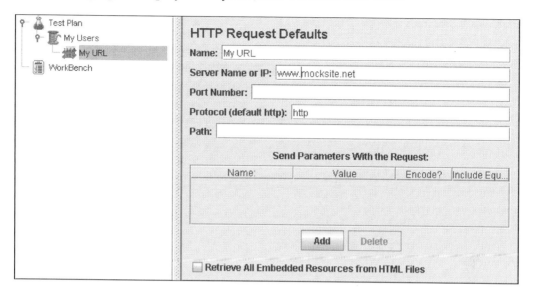

- **Add HTTP Requests**

    In this step, we will make two mock HTTP requests from the target server: the default page and another page from the same URL. As JMeter executes elements in the order that they appear in the Test Plan tree, we will add the request for the default page first.

    1. Right-click the **My Users** Thread element. Select **Add | Sampler | HTTP Request**.

    2. Select the **HTTP Request** element in the left panel and make the changes as follows:

        a. **Name** field: **Home Page**

        b. **Web Server** section: This information has been specified in HTTP Request Defaults. There is no need to edit this section, unless you need to redirect to a different path than that specified in the HTTP Request Default.

        c. **Path** field: **/**

            - Since we have specified the **Server name** in the HTTP Request Default element, we do not need to add anything more to this field.

The following figure displays how your JMeter should now look:

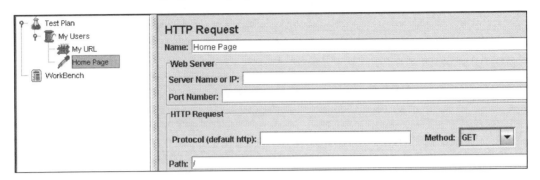

3. Add another HTTP Request element below the **Home Page** element and make changes as follows:

   a. **Name** field: **Sample Page**

   b. **Path** field: **/sample.html** (or a known path to your own sample URL)

   - Since we have specified the Server name in the HTTP Request Default element as www.mocksite.com, this path will be appended to create the complete path to target the page.

The following figure displays how your JMeter should now look:

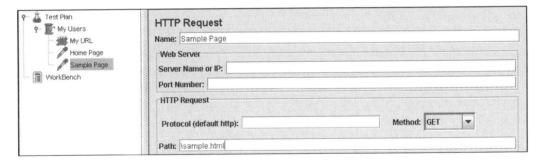

- **Add a Listener**

  Finally, we will add a simple Listener, Aggregate Report. This element will store all result of your HTTP Requests and will display the statistical information in a table form.

  1. Select the **My Users** element and select **Add | Listener | Aggregate Report**. This will be added as the last element.

2. In the **Write All Data to a File** section: in the **Filename** field type the name of the directory or select the directory in which the file will be saved using the **Browse** button and type in filename of the output file.

The following figure displays how your JMeter should now look:

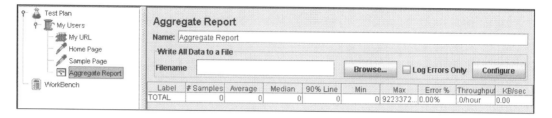

- **Save & Run the Test Plan**

JMeter requires us to save a Test Plan before running it.

1. Select **Save Test Plan** from the **File** menu. JMeter lets you save portions or branches of a Test Plan by simply selecting the element where a branch begins.

2. At **Save as**, type in the filename. For this example, type **My Users**. The extension will be set at .jmx.

3. From the **Run** menu, select **Run**.

The following figure is how your **Aggregate Report Element** and **Control Panel** should look as it runs. Notice that there is a small gray square in the upper right-hand corner. The number beside it shows the number of active threads vs. total threads.

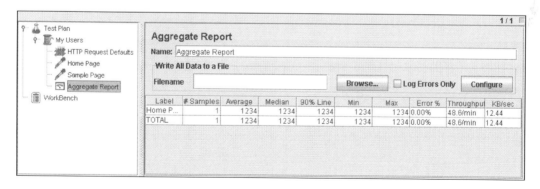

Following is what your **Aggregate Report** Element and Control Panel should look like after completing running the Test Plan. It is only when the whole thread has completed, that it returns to grey. You may also manually stop the run by selecting **Stop** from the **Run** menu.

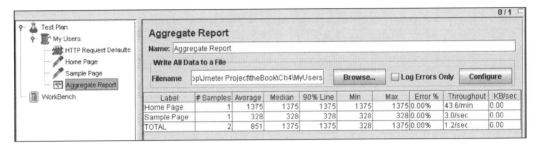

The column headings are explained briefly as follows:

- **Label** — The label of the sample
- **# Samples** — The number of samples for the URL
- **Average** — The mean time of a set of results
- **Median** — The time in the middle of a set of results
- **90% Line** — The maximum time taken for the fastest 90% of the samples
- **Min** — The lowest time for the samples
- **Max** — The longest time for the samples
- **Error %** — Percent of requests with errors or failures
- **Throughput** — Throughput measured in requests per unit of time
- **Kb/sec** — The throughput measured in Kilobytes per second

For this example, we are running only one sample for each page. Therefore, the average is equivalent to the median value, while min time is equivalent to max time. These figures will differ if the Thread Group simulates two or more samples per page following the Configuration set in the Thread Group.

Summary

JMeter provides visible tools (or elements) that allow us to capture information about the application we are testing and to save and view the results in various formats. I find this very supportive of the heavy documentation that a testing requires for most of the time. The visual information JMeter provides us makes it easier to evaluate the success/failure of our testing. As it allows us to save portions (or branches) of a Test Plan individually, we can certainly reuse them as we merge with other Test Plans. This is an embodiment of Java, the object-oriented language used to develop JMeter.

At this point, you already have a better idea about the working of JMeter. We will extend this Test Plan in the next chapters to include elements and properties that allow us to do performance testing and functional testing of web applications. Once you are familiar with the functions of these elements, next important question to ask yourself is what do you want to test out of your application? The next step is to find out which JMeter elements would best suit those testing needs. These questions and more will be further explored in the next two chapters.

5

Load/Performance Testing
of Websites

So you are ready now to take on Web Load/Performance Testing on your target web application.

Before we embark on this significant journey, I am obliged to highlight the fact that load testing and performance testing do somewhat differ. IEEE 90 defines Performance Testing as, *Testing conducted to evaluate the compliance of a system or component with specified performance requirements.* Some of its goals include to identify bottlenecks in a system, finding which can later support performance tuning efforts, to aid in auditing the system's performance, and/or to collect other relevant data to help stakeholders make informed decisions related to the quality of the application under test.

Load Testing, being a part of performance testing, is simply the process of subjecting a component or a whole system to a work level approaching its limits. Another point of concern is that some quarters use load testing interchangeably with stress testing. This may not be an entirely accurate practice, as there is a thin line between these two terms. Load testing is performed within the capacity of the resource(s) being subjected, while stress testing is normally performed to evaluate the performance of resources and behavior at or beyond normal capacity. In summary, both load testing and stress testing are part of what makes performance testing.

For sake of argument (and so as not to overwhelm you—the reader), this chapter will focus on using JMeter to perform Web Application Load Testing as being a part of Performance Testing. First, it will give you some general guides to help you prepare and plan for a load test. The remaining part of the chapter will give you a step-by-step walkthrough in bringing together JMeter components to build a load-test plan. The final section of this chapter will capture the test results after running the test.

Preparing for Load Testing

In preparing for load testing it is utterly important to address a number of concerns with regards to the target server under test. As load testing helps to benchmark performance behavior of a server, it is important to be able to identify the general expectations and other matters that would normally be taken into account in order to carry out a successful load testing.

What You Need to Know

As noted earlier, load testing in this matter subjects the application server to work approaching its limits. Obviously, the limits will need to be clearly defined, understood, and agreed upon by the stakeholders, namely your superior(s). In addition, performance metrics need to be clear in order to keep the performance goals in check.

Important expectations as for any load testing include:

- A suitable time to load-test the application, for instance when no development work is taking place on the server (load testing may cause the server to crash) and/or no other users are accessing the server (else the testing results would not yield the correct measures)
- The performance metrics, accepted levels, or SLAs and goals
- Objectives of the test
- The Internet protocol(s) the application is(are) using (HTTPS, HTTP, FTP, etc.)
- If your application has a state, the method used to manage it (URL rewriting, cookies, etc.)
- The workload at normal time and at peak time

It is often advisable that any form of performance testing, inclusive of load testing, is performed on a functionally stable application, regardless of the environment where the application is located. Load testing is best done when the functionality of the **Application Under Test (AUT)** is stable enough to yield consistent and correct results.

Some Helpful Tips to Get Better Results

- Use meaningful test scenarios (use cases are helpful) to construct test plans with 'real-life' test cases.
- Run JMeter on a machine other than that running the application you are testing.

- Make sure that the machine running JMeter has sufficient network bandwidth, so the network connection has little to no impact on the results. Also, the machine running JMeter should have enough computing power (memory, CPU) to generate load.

- Let JMeter Test Plan run for long time periods, hours or days, or for a large number of iterations. This may yield a smaller standard deviation, giving better average results. In addition, this practice may test system availability rate and may highlight any decay in server performance.

- Ensure that the application is stable and optimized for one user before testing it for concurrent users.

- Incorporate 'thinking time' or delays using Timers in your JMeter Test Plan.

- Conduct tests under a monitored and controlled environment, to prevent other users from affecting JMeter results.

- Keep a close watch on the four main things: processor, memory, disk, and network.

- Only run JMeter against servers that you are assigned to test, else you may be accused of causing DoS attacks.

Using JMeter Components

For practical and realistic reasons, we will use an existing remote server to test its performance. First of all, we will create some useful scenarios as the baseline of our test.

First, we will need to determine the test cases. Generally, we will test five key scenarios:

1. **Homepage**
2. **Keyword Search** — New Visitor making a keyword search
3. **Create Account** — New Visitor creating an Account
4. **Select A Title** — Registered Visitor selecting a featured title
5. **Add To Cart** — Registered Visitor adding selection to cart

These scenarios will be included in a single JMeter Test Plan, for simplicity reasons.

Recording HTTP Requests

A fast way to capture the HTTP pages of this application is to record every request made to the server. For this we will need to use a special-purpose Configuration Element: HTTP Proxy Server. Note that the Proxy Server element is only available in the Workbench element.

Since Proxy Server element records any page requests, besides user requests, it will also record background requests made by the browser as modern browsers do. As we would like the Proxy element to record only requests to the target server, consider setting web filter to allow the current browser to make requests only to that server. Otherwise, unnecessary requests will only clutter your recording. You may find these web filters as an option in any Internet security tool or software currently running on your machine.

Run JMeter (double-click `JMeter.bat` from `jmeter/bin` folder). You will see the default Elements, which are **Test Plan** and **Workbench**. Right-click on **Workbench** and select **Add | Non Test Elements | HTTP Proxy Server**.

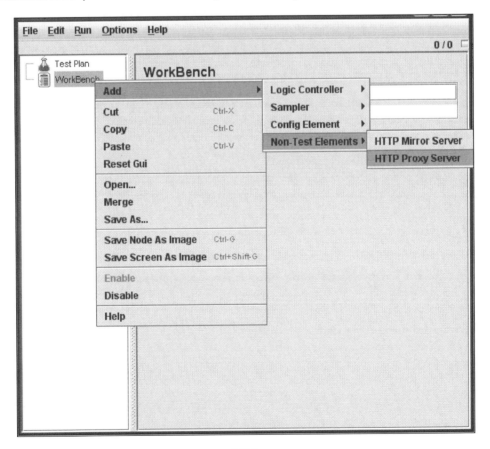

An HTTP Proxy Server configuration Element will appear as a child of WorkBench. Bear in mind that child elements of WorkBench are not saved as part of Test Plan, but you can save them separately. In the HTTP Proxy server configuration Target Controller lets you determine where the recorded requests will be placed and the Grouping option allows the recorded pages to be grouped or left as individual requests. *Notice that the port we are using is the default port, following the browser setting in the next instructions.*

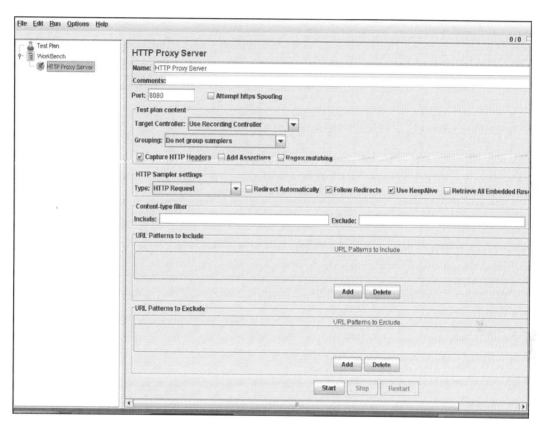

Next, we will change the setting of your favorite browser to access a proxy (in our case JMeter HTTP Proxy), listening to the same port. You may also use port 90 for both the browser and JMeter Proxy setting.

The following figure shows the setting for Mozilla Firefox:

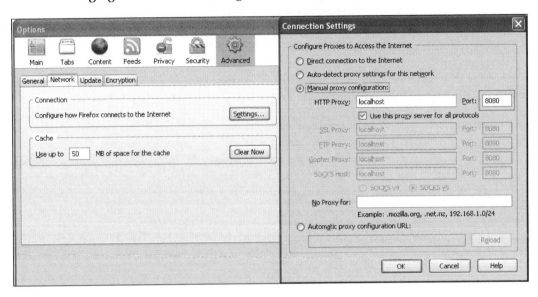

The following screenshot shows the setting for IE:

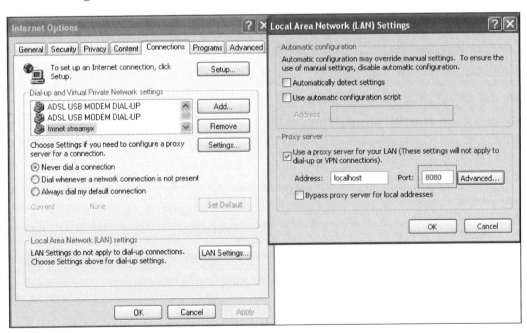

We are expecting that a single page request will make several embedded requests for images, JavaScript files, CSS files, etc. Therefore for a more managed recording, it is a good practice to create controllers that can contain the sub-requests for each request.

Right-click on **HTTP Proxy Server** and select **Add | Logic Controller | Simple Controller**. Repeat so we have five Controllers, or you can simply copy and paste. Name each Controller: **Homepage**, **Keyword Search**, **Create Account**, **Select Title**, and **Add to Cart**. Then configure the Target Controller to **HTTP Proxy Server | Homepage**, while the other defaults remain.

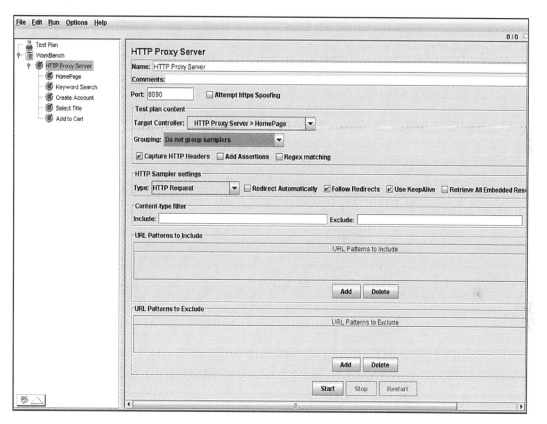

Now we are ready to record our first page request. As we return to JMeter, simply press the **Start** button at the Element Controller, and use your browser. Remember that JMeter records all HTTP requests from the browser you are using; therefore, with all the rich browsers and with all the add-ons we have today, you might want to filter that only requests to the targeted server are allowed. You may configure your browser or firewall to do so.

Click the **Start** button, and type the **URL** of the server you want to test in the Address bar. You will see that JMeter has begun to record the request to the homepage and its sub-requests into Homepage Controller.

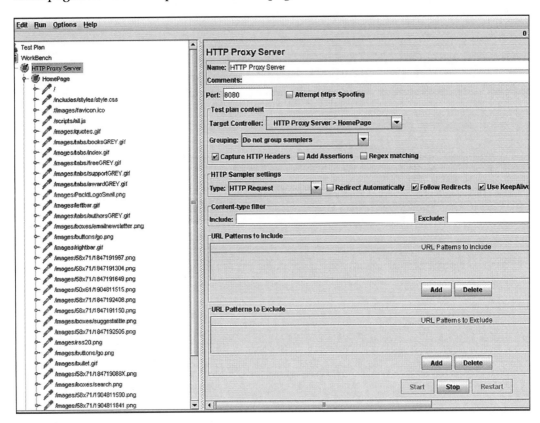

Next, on the Target Controller, select **HTTP Proxy Server | Keyword Search**, return to the browser and type in a keyword and click search. JMeter will record the following search page and its sub-requests in the **Keyword Search** Controller and nowhere else.

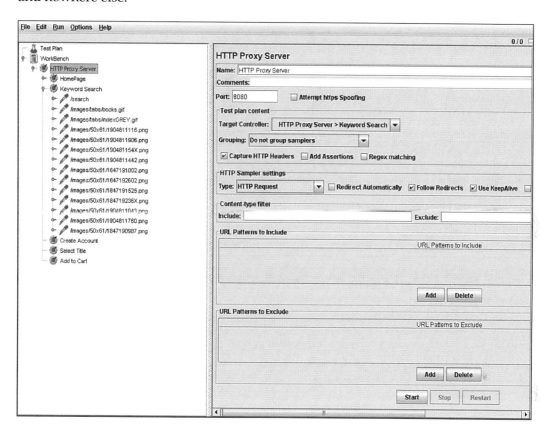

Repeat for the **Create Account**, **Select Title**, and **Add to Cart** Controllers, switching to the respective Target Controllers.

The final recording screenshot is as shown in the following figure:

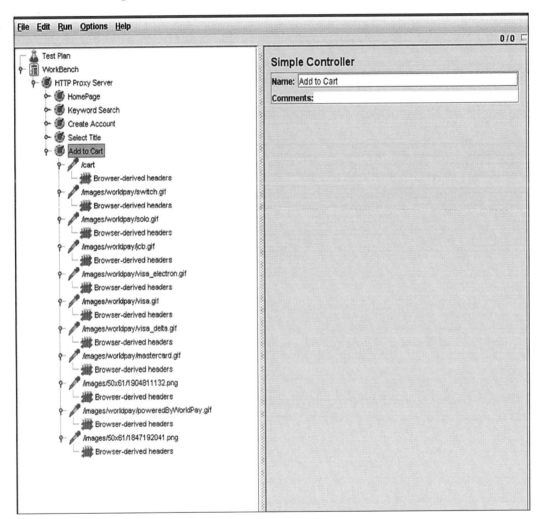

Once the recording is over, we will save these by right-clicking on the **HTTP Proxy Server** Controller and saving it in a folder of your choice. As you will see, each request may or may not generate sub-requests for files. The caching feature of today's web browsers allows these files (*.png, *.jpg, *.css, *.js, etc.) to be stored in the browser's cache the first time they are downloaded. Unless there were changes in the main request, the browser will not make new requests for these cached files as it will simply load them from the local cache. How is this feature helpful in benchmarking the performance of an application? To iterate, this has become a test goal decision to make whether the application should be tested to evaluate performance for first-time visitors or existing visitors. If we are testing for first-time visitors, we can use the first recording to simulate first-time users. Subsequent recordings can be used to simulate existing users.

Alternatively, we can configure the Proxy Server Configuration Element to exclude recording of particular file type(s), as the following figure indicates.

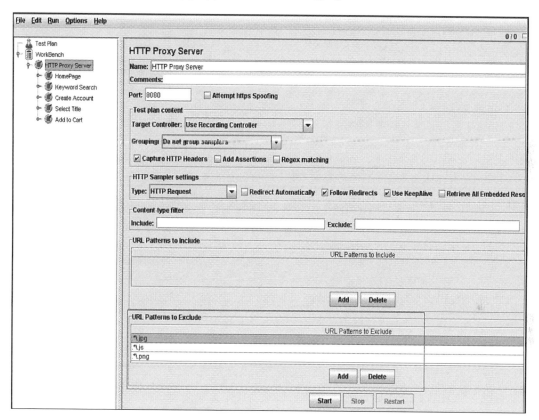

Subsequent recording of similar actions using the new configuration of HTTP Proxy Server will exclude the caching files. Let us perform another round of recording and see how that turns out. The following screenshot highlights the first and second round of recording.

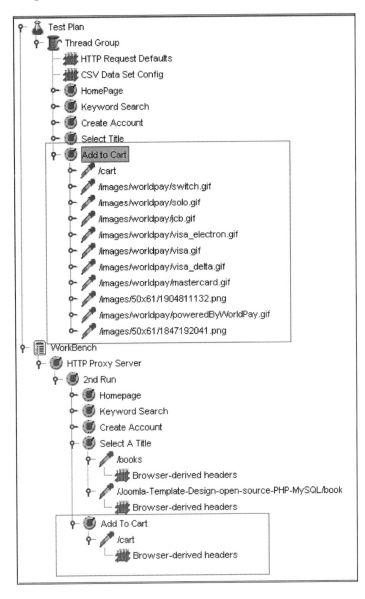

For our purpose, we will simulate 10 existing visitors, while running the test plan for a minimum of 10 iterations, with a think time between one and three seconds. We will use the second recording too, as it is the closest to emulate existing visitors, as we would expect that the caching files would have already been stored locally. To remove elements, highlight the Controllers in the Test Plan and press delete. To move the new Controllers to the Test Plan, simply highlight and Copy Paste in the Thread Group.

Creating the Test Plan

We will begin by creating a single Thread Group (Users Group) that we will configure later as we expand the Test Plan.

Right-click on the **Test Plan element** and select **Add | Thread Group**. A Thread Group Element will appear. Configure the **Number of Threads** *to* **10**, **Ramp-Up Period** *to* **1 second**, and **Loop Count** *to* **50**. If you wish, you can set the **Scheduler** so your test plan can run automatically on the pre-determined time and date.

We want each request to target only one server, therefore, we set a request default to serve this purpose. Add to the **Test Plan Config Element | HTTP Request Defaults**:

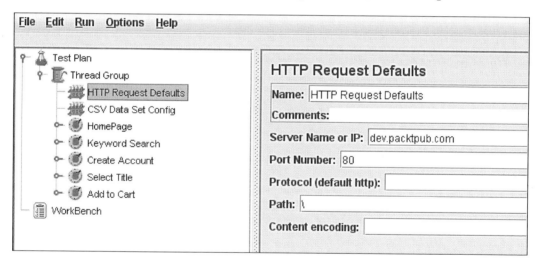

As this test should emulate real-life scenarios, this test requires that 500 unique accounts be created at the **Create Account** Request. Since we will need to generate multiple new users as JMeter creates 'new' accounts, one option is to parse unique account pairs into the appropriate Sampler, in this case the \login request in the **Create An Account** Controller. JMeter provides this capability by **Pre-Processor | User Parameter Element** or **Config Element | CSV Data Set Config**. The **User Parameter Element** allows the user to specify unique values for User Variables specific to individual threads. The **CSV Data Set Config** element serves the same purpose; however, these values are read from lines from a file, and split into variables that later can be used throughout the life of the thread.

For providing a large number of users, CSV Data Set Config would be a better choice. The following figure will compare both the elements.

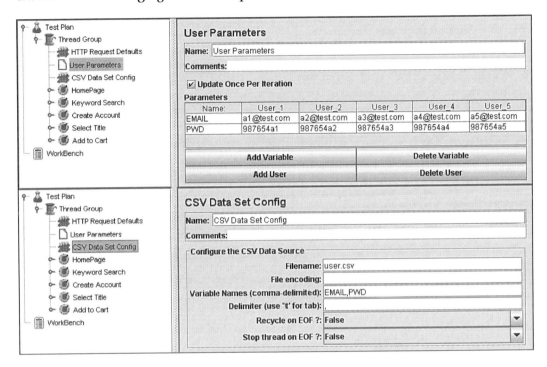

Since we need to create 500 unique accounts, the natural choice would be using **CSV Data Set Config Element**. It is advisable that the CSV file created for this test be located in the same directory as the Test Plan. This element gives you the option to define the delimiter of your data file. Since we want only these 500 unique accounts created and nothing more, we do not choose **recycle on EOF**, which would reread these pairs from the beginning of thr file once the whole file is parsed.

These data will need to be parsed into the appropriate parameter(s) using the function syntax: ${VARIABLE-Name}. We will use these account pairs in **Create Account | /login Sampler** where you see the corresponding variable names or parameters (email, password, confirm password) are captured in the Sampler. In the following figure you may notice the **Value** for these parameters corresponds with Variable Names defined earlier in the CSV Data Set Config Element.

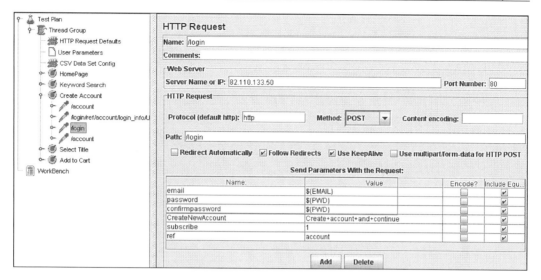

Adding Listeners

We are now ready to add Listeners to our Test Plan. As we are evaluating performance based on scenarios, each scenario Controller will have its own Listener. One Listener is sufficient to capture the performance data, as the saved data can be represented in various ways according to the Listener selected to view these data. The following steps will give you a better walk through.

Right-click on the **Homepage** Controller and select **Add | Listener | View Results in Table**. In the Filename text-field simply type the name of the XML or JTL file, along with its extension, that will store the results for the requests in this Controller. By default this will be located in the \bin folder of your JMeter installation path; however, you may choose to specify a different location. Follow similar steps for all other Controllers.

Adding Timers

As we are emulating real-life visitors/users, we will need to consider delays between requests. Such delay is also known as **think time**, which a real user will take as he/she will need to decide the next action, be it a click to some other link, or pressing some button, etc. that causes a new request to the target server.

To add a Timer, right-click on the element for which we want to simulate the think-time, select **Add | Timer**, and choose the type of timer. For this exercise, we will configure the two timers we are using, **Uniform Random timer** and **Constant timer**, to emulate real-user actions as closely as possible. 'Uniform Random' timer pauses each sampler request for a random amount of time, with each time interval having the same probability of occurring. The total delay is the sum of the random value and the offset value. Meanwhile, 'Constant timer' allows the thread to pause for the same amount of time between requests.

The following screenshots explain the above paragraph.

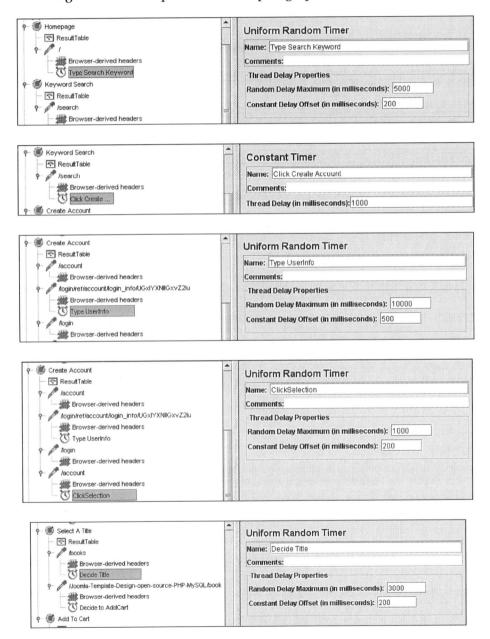

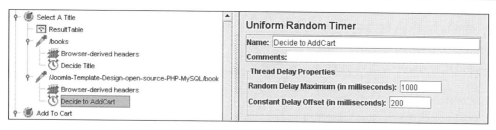

We may need to organize the Test Plan tree, by placing sub-requests of a request Sampler as children of the Sampler, so that we can measure the performance better according to particular actions of a user. To view the Results for all Samplers, we may add a Summary Listener of the scope of the Test Plan and configure the Filename so the test summary data is saved separately. The final Test Plan may look as in the following snapshot:

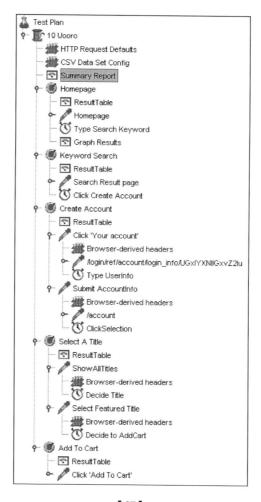

Running the Test Plan

We are now ready to run the Test plan we have built. We may rename the Thread Group to "10 Users" for better documentation. Look at the tiny gray indicator box at the top right of the Control Panel. The numbers beside the box indicate number of active threads vs. total number of threads in the Thread Group.

JMeter requires saving the Test Plan before running; unless indicated otherwise, it will save the Test Plan in the \bin folder of your JMeter installation path. To run the Test Plan, go to the **Run** menu and select **Start**. As soon as it runs, the gray box will turn green as JMeter ramps up the total number of active threads to 10. You will see that JMeter takes approximately 5 seconds to activate the total number of users with a delay of 100ms (1000ms per 10 users) between subsequent threads. This demonstrates the 1 second ramp-up time we have set in Thread Group earlier.

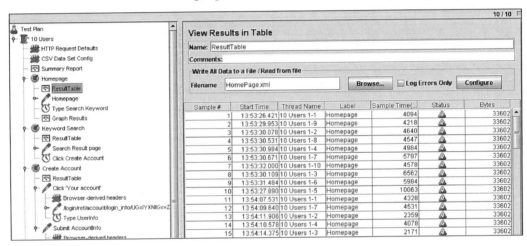

When the test is complete, the indicator box will return to gray.

Interpreting the Results

Once the test is completed, we can now retrieve the results we have saved for each Controller. With the exception of the Assertion Result Listener, the saved data can be viewed in numerous forms. Let us use HomePage.xml as our specimen dataset. Add more Listeners to this Controller: Summary Report, Aggregate Result, and Graph Results. To retrieve the results for this Sampler, type in the name of the file to which you saved data for this Sampler, and press *Enter*. The following snapshots show the result views.

For **Graph Results**, the **Data** legend shows us the widely dispersed data, representing the large value of the Standard **Deviation** across all samples for this Homepage Sampler. In the case where the results are highly skewed or not symmetrical using 'mean' would result in inaccurate representation of response time. The **Median** value, which is found in Aggregate Report and Graph Results would closely approximate the response time.

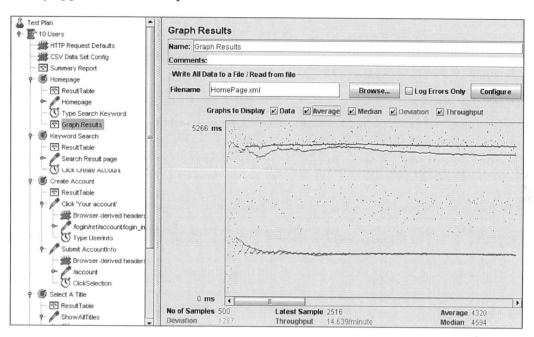

The saved results can be viewed in various forms. The following snapshot is of the saved test result viewed using the **Summary Report** Listener.

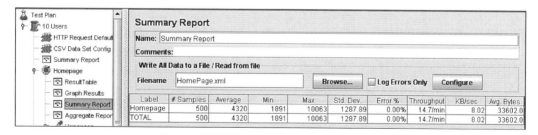

The following snapshot is of the saved test result viewed using the **Aggregate Report** Listener. Note that Summary Report and Aggregate Report display the same set of test results differently, following different computation over the same data.

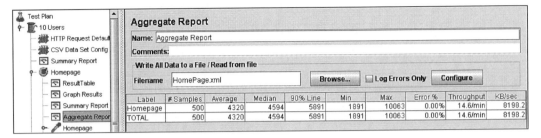

In the case where data distribution is even, or follows the 'bell' distribution, median and average will have the same or only slightly different values. We can see the data distribution pattern by adding a **Spline Visualizer** Listener using the filename of the file used to store the sampler results. The following shows us the distribution graph for requests to this page.

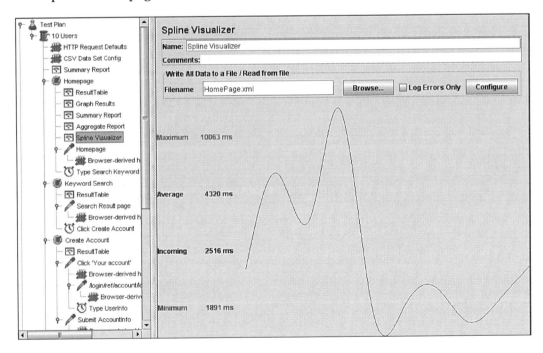

In this test, we can approximate that for the 10 simultaneous users, the approximate response time would be the median figure, since the data is widely spread.

How do we measure the point at which the server's performance degrades, or bottlenecks may appear? This important key question may be resolved if we run several thread groups that represent increasing number of 'Users', for example 10, 50, 100 users or even 500 or more for a large-scale, mission-critical server. We can then identify the points where performance degradation begins taking place. These User groups can be placed in the same Test Plan, or in a separate Test Plan, while maintaining the default configurations. This sort of practice allows us to benchmark the server's performance to find the bottlenecks in the server, hence creating a baseline for future tests.

Our test, however, does not seem to show any performance degradation, simply because it is running only a handful of users almost simultaneously. We run the test for 50 times so that we can get a better shot at the figures, in case failed requests occur, which normally would happen in real-life. You may want to expand the Test Plan further to include 50, 100, or even 500 users to find out if any performance degradation could occur.

With an average of 4.3 and median of 4.5 seconds, its speed of response is generally acceptable as it meets the threshold of acceptability for retail web page response times. See `http://www.akamai.com/html/about/press/releases/2006/press_110606.html` for more insight on this finding.

You may find that this analysis is limited as it yields results for only a minimum number of scenarios and concurrent users. But fear not, there are plenty more analyses you can make out of your future tests, if you create larger Thread groups, and maybe opt for stress testing and/or monitoring the server for performance.

Remote Testing with JMeter

Although this chapter does not give further details about stress testing your target server, this topic may capture your interest. This remote testing capability is very useful when your machine alone may have performance issues as it tries to simulate a very large number of concurrent users. This may well affect the speed and frequency of requests made to the target server, therefore affecting testing goals and subsequently, the results.

For more details on this attractive feature, you may refer to the online manual on remote testing on `http://jakarta.apache.org/jmeter/usermanual/remote-test.html`. JMeter Wiki also provides a simple and easy to follow guide (PDF)—`http://jakarta.apache.org/jmeter/usermanual/jmeter_distributed_testing_step_by_step.pdf`.

These guiding documents highlight following settings and configurations. You may remotely assign 'slave' machines to make requests to the target server while your machine becomes the 'master'. In other words, one machine controls the execution of the specified JMeter tests, as the results are collected at the 'master' machine. This approach lets us benchmark the target server's performance even more closely and effectively than otherwise.

Monitoring the Server's Performance

There is a special Listener that allows you to monitor the target server's performance as Samplers make requests. However, this Monitor Result Listener is designed to work with Apache Tomcat, and only Apache Tomcat application server version 5 and above. You may refer to http://jakarta.apache.org/jmeter/usermanual/ build-monitor-test-plan.html to find out more. For any other application server, you may use any other available open-source tools, or commercial tools.

The following are snapshots of the **Monitor Result** Listener, taken from JMeter's official user manual. The **Health** tab shows the general status of one or more servers.

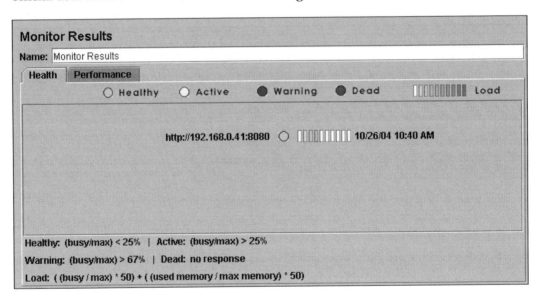

This snapshot from the **Performance** tab of this Listener displays the specific performance indicators for the selected server affected by a load test for the last 1000 samples. These graphs indicate the general health of the server (green), the load capacity that the server was able to process (blue), ratio of server memory being utilized—free vs. total memory (yellow), and thread ratio capacity (red).

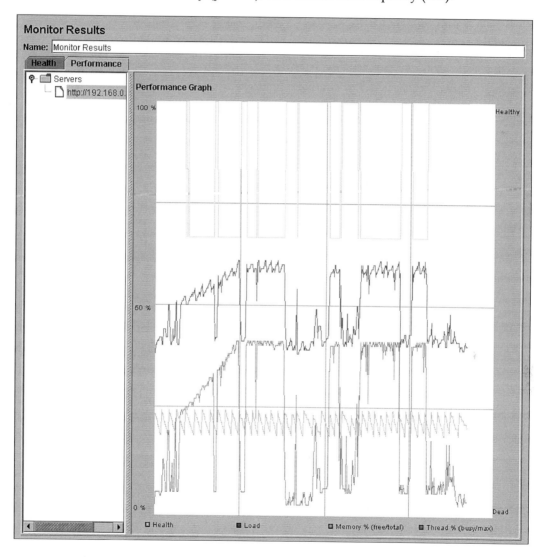

Summary

This test helps us to find out if the performance goals and/or SLA are reached given the total threads and scenarios. As we highlight the key pages of the website/application, JMeter running our Test Plan allows us to use the mean or median response time, depending on the type of data distribution, to approximate how fast the target server responds to concurrent requests. If the target server is Tomcat 5.0 or above, then you can easily monitor the server's general health in terms of its computing resources, such as memory use, workload, etc. As you explore JMeter's capability for remote testing, you can conveniently extend your Test Plan to support stress testing purposes as well. The following chapter will also make use of the Test Plan that we have just built to support functional testing—a real time-saver.

6

Functional Testing

JMeter is found to be very useful and convenient in support of functional testing. Although JMeter is known more as a performance testing tool, functional testing elements can be integrated within the Test Plan, which was originally designed to support load testing. Many other load-testing tools provide little or none of this feature, restricting themselves to performance-testing purposes. Besides integrating functional-testing elements along with load-testing elements in the Test Plan, you can also create a Test Plan that runs these exclusively. In other words, aside from creating a Load Test Plan, JMeter also allows you to create a **Functional Test Plan**. This flexibility is certainly resource-efficient for the testing project.

This chapter will give a walkthrough on how to create a Test Plan as we incorporate and/or configure JMeter elements to support functional testing. This chapter assumes that you have successfully gone through Chapter 5, and created a Test Plan for a specific target web server. We will begin the chapter with a quick overview to prepare you with a few expectations about JMeter. Later, we will create a new Test Plan similar to the Test Plan in Chapter 5, only smaller. The Test Plan we will create and run at the end of this chapter will incorporate elements that support functional testing, exclusively.

Preparing for Functional Testing

In this regard, I need to highlight that JMeter does not have a built-in browser, unlike many functional-test tools. It tests on the protocol layer, not the client layer (i.e. JavaScripts, applets, etc.) and it does not render the page for viewing. Although, by default that embedded resources can be downloaded, rendering these in the **Listener | View Results Tree** may not yield a 100% browser-like rendering. In fact, it may not be able to render large HTML files at all. This makes it difficult to test the GUI of an application under testing.

However, to compensate for these shortcomings, JMeter allows the tester to create assertions based on the tags and text of the page as the HTML file is received by the client. With some knowledge of HTML tags, you can test and verify any elements as you would expect them in the browser.

Unlike for a load-testing Test Plan, it is unnecessary to select a specific workload time to perform a functional test. In fact, the application you want to test may even reside locally, with your own machine acting as the "localhost" server for your web application. For this chapter, we will limit ourselves to selected functional aspects of the page that we seek to verify or assert.

Using JMeter Components

We will create a Test Plan in order to demonstrate how we can configure the Test Plan to include functional testing capabilities. The modified Test Plan will include these scenarios:

1. **Create Account** — New Visitor creating an Account
2. **Log in User** — User logging in to an Account

Following these scenarios, we will simulate various entries and form submission as a request to a page is made, while checking the correct page response to these user entries. We will add assertions to the samples following these scenarios to verify the 'correctness' of a requested page. In this manner, we can see if the pages responded correctly to invalid data. For example, we would like to check that the page responded with the correct warning message when a user enters an invalid password, or whether a request returns the correct page.

First of all, we will create a series of test cases following the various user actions in each scenario. The test cases may be designed as follows:

CREATE ACCOUNT

Test Steps	Data	Expected
1 **Go to Home page.**	www.packtpub.com	Home page loads and renders with no page error
2 **Click Your Account link** (top right).	User action	1. **Your Account** page loads and renders with no page error. 2. **Logout** link is not found.

Test Steps	Data	Expected
3 **No Password:** - Enter email address in **Email** text field. - Click the **Create Account and Continue** button.	email=EMAIL	1. Your Account page resets with Warning message—**Please enter password.** 2. **Logout** link not found.
4 **Short Password:** - Enter email address in **Email** text field. - Enter password in **Password** text field. - Enter password in **Confirm Password** text field. - Click **Create Account and Continue** button.	email=EMAIL password= SHORT_PWD confirm password= SHORT_PWD	1. Your Account page resets with Warning message—**Your password must be 8 characters or longer.** 2. **Logout** link is not found.
5 **Unconfirmed Password:** - Enter email address in **Email** text field. - Enter password in **Password** text field. - Enter password in **Confirm Password** text field. - Click **Create Account and Continue** button.	email=EMAIL password= VALID_PWD confirm password= INVALID_PWD	1. Your Account page resets with Warning message**Password does not match.** 2. **Logout** link is not found.
6 **Register Valid User:** - Enter email address in **Email** text field. - Enter password in **Password** text field. - Enter password in **Confirm Password** text field. - Click **Create Account and Continue** button.	email=EMAIL password= VALID_PWD confirm password= VALID_PWD	1. **Logout** link is found. 2. Page redirects to User Account page. 3. Message found: **You are registered as: e:<EMAIL>.**
7 **Click Logout link.**	User action	1. **Logout** link is NOT found.

LOGIN USER

Test Steps	Data	Expected
1 **Click Home page.**	User action	1. **WELCOME** tab is active.
2 **Log in Wrong Password:** - Enter email in **Email** text field - Enter password at **Password** text field. - Click **Login** button.	email=EMAIL password= INVALID_PWD	1. **Logout** link is NOT found. 2. Page refreshes. 3. Warning message—**Sorry your password was incorrect** appears.

	Test Steps	Data	Expected
3	**Log in Non-Exist Account:** - Enter email in **Email** text field. - Enter password in **Password** text field. - Click **Login** button.	email= INVALID_ EMAIL password= INVALID_PWD	1. **Logout** link is NOT found. 2. Page refreshes. 3. Warning message — **Sorry, this does not match any existing accounts. Please check your details and try again or open a new account below** appears.
4	**Log in Valid Account:** - Enter email in **Email** text field. - Enter password in Password text field. - Click **Login**-button.	email=EMAIL password= VALID_PWD	1. **Logout** link is found. 2. Page reloads. 3. Login successful message — **You are logged in as:** appears.
5	**Click Logout link.**	User action	1. **Logout** link is NOT found.

With the exception of the Configuration elements, Listeners, and Assertions, which we will add later, our **Test Plan** will take the form that you see in the following screenshot:

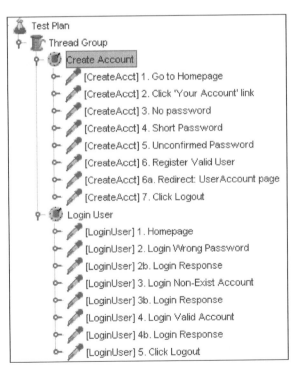

Using HTTP Proxy Server to Record Page Requests

As in recording requests in Chapter 5, you will need to include the HTTP Proxy Server element in the WorkBench. Some configuration will be required, as shown in the following snapshot:

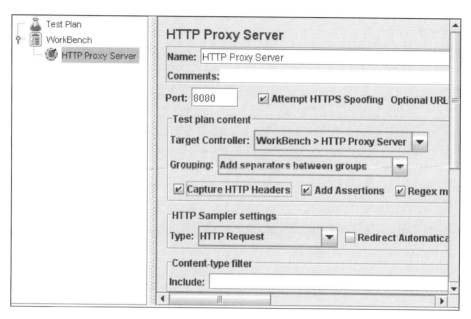

Configuring the Proxy Server

Simulating **Create Account** and **Login User** scenarios will require JMeter to make requests for the registration and login pages that are exposed via HTTPS. By default, **HTTP Proxy Server** is unable to record HTTP requests. However, we can override this by selecting (checking) the **Attempt HTTPS Spoofing** checkbox.

Selecting **Add Assertion** will be especially useful as we add specific patterns of the page that we want to evaluate as a later part of this exercise. The **Capture HTTP Headers** option is selected to capture the Header information as we begin recording. However, to make the recording neater, we will keep this option unchecked.

In addition, since we do not require images in our testing, in the **URL Pattern to Exclude** section, add these patterns: `.*\.jpg`, `.*\.js`, `.*\.png`, `.*\.gif'`, `.*\.ico`, `.*\.css`, otherwise these image files, which are not necessary for our testing, will be recorded causing unnecessary clutter in our recording.

Adding HTTP Request Default

A useful addition to this element is the HTTP Request Default element, a type of Configuration element. Since this Test Plan will employ multiple HTTP request elements targeting the same server and port, this element will be very useful. The web server name will not be captured for each HTTP Request sampler record, since the Request Default element will retain this information. With a little configuration change in this element, it allows the Test Plan to run even when the application is the deployed to a different server and/or port. The following snapshot is the **HTTP Request Default** element that we will use for this exercise.

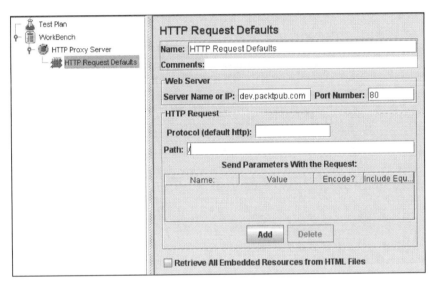

As we use this default element, our subsequent recording never needs to append the Server name. The result of our recording of the first page is shown in the following snapshot:

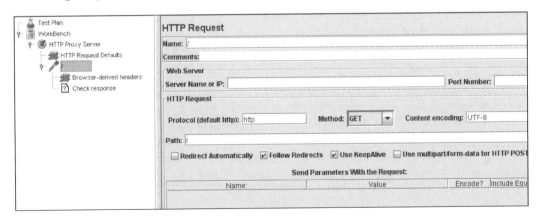

Adding HTTP Header Manager

Another very useful default element is the **HTTP Header Manager** Configuration element. This element can either be added to the Test Plan and configured manually as an afterthought, or we can simply use the recorded **Browser-derived headers** element as included in the recording. For convenience, we will choose the latter option. Once the Proxy Server records the homepage request, stop the recording. You will find a Header Manager for this page is being captured, as **Browser-derived header**. Simply click and drag this element to the top of the current scope of the HTTP Proxy Server. Notice that I have removed the **Referer**, since we want to create a default for the remaining HTTP Requests. Following is a snapshot of this change.

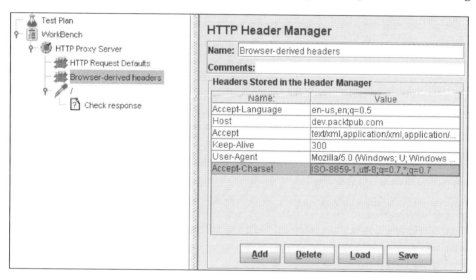

Now you may de-select the **Capture HTTP Headers** option in the Proxy Server element, since we have the default header.

Let the Recording Begin...

Let us proceed with the recording following the test cases in the previous table as our guide. As you record each page, select the specific tags or page elements the correctness of which you want to validate and add them to the **Patterns to Test** section in the **Response Assertion** element of each sampler. This may take most of your recording time, since as you record, you need to decide carefully which page element(s) would be the most effective measure of correctness. There are plenty of developer tools available to help you in this possibly tedious task. My favorite is the **Inspect Element** feature in **Firebug**, a Firefox browser add-on by Mozilla. You may choose patterns that you would expect to see or otherwise by selecting or de-selecting the **Not** option at **Pattern Matching Rules** section.

After recording is completed, you may rename and organize your samplers, as you move them to the Test Plan (refer to the following figure). You may want to add a few more Configuration elements in your Test Plan, as in my sample shown in the following snapshot:

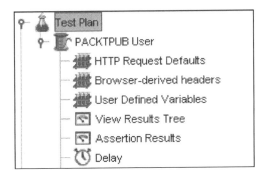

- I have added User Defined Variables, two more Listeners, and a Constant Timer with a constant delay of 2 seconds after the request for each page was completed. The Assertion Results listener is used with the Response Assertion elements, to summarize the success or failure of a page in meeting the validation criteria defined in each Response Assertion.

Adding User Defined Variables

The **User Defined Variables** (**UDV**) element as shown in the following snapshot is particularly interesting with regards to the test case design we drafted earlier in the table. It allows you to plug values to variables being used in various locations in the Test Plan. The JMeter Test Plan we have created will implement the exact values assigned to different variables. Following is a snapshot of the UDV I have set up for our Test Plan.

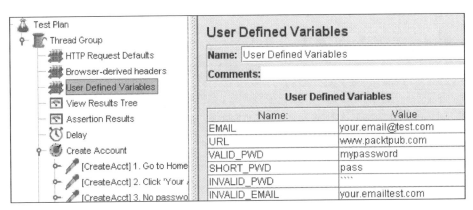

How do we use these variables in the Test Plan? Simply use the format ${Variable-name} anywhere in the Test Plan that we want to use the value of a Variable.

For example, in the HTTP Request Sampler following **CREATE ACCOUNT | Test Step#6: Register Valid User**, as you can see below, the parameter **password** has value ${VALID_PWD}, referring to the corresponding variable assigned in UDV.

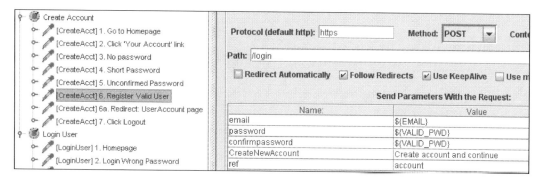

We may also use the variables set in UDV in other elements, namely Response Assertions. This feature is particularly useful when the assertion depends on varying values, such as when we want to verify URLs, verifying user names, account no, etc. — depending on the values we want to include throughout the entire testing. The following snapshot may give us a clear idea of how a UDV can be used in an Assertion element. The URL variable defined in UDV is used in the **Patterns to Test** section of this Assertion, as part of a complete page element that we want to verify in the page Sampler.

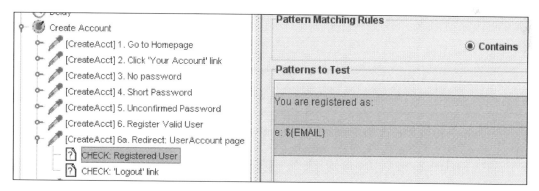

Running the Test

Once the assertions are properly completed, we are expecting that running our Test Plan would pass all the assertions. Passed assertions will not show any error in **Assertion Results | Listener** installed within the same scope. As for all Listeners, results as captured by the Listeners can be saved and reproduced at a later time. Following is a sample explaining what passed Assertions would reveal as the Test is executed.

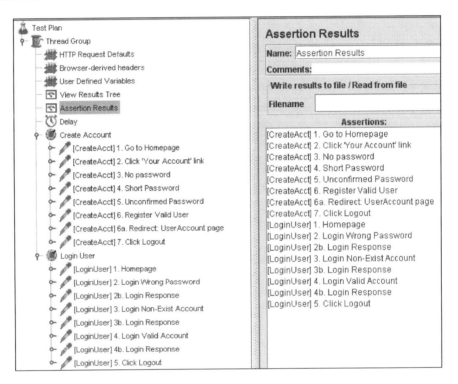

On the other hand, a failed Assertion would show an error message in the same Listener as the following snapshot illustrates.

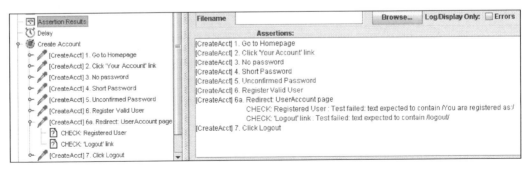

Since a page error or **Page not found** error is a real risk in web applications, a failure may originate from such an error, and not just because of a failed Assertion. We can view more information about the sampler that contains the failed Assertion to investigate the origins of a failure. A **View Results Tree** Listener records the details of requests and logs all errors (indicated by the red warning sign and red fonts).

The following figure shows that the page was available and page request was successful, however, the assertion failed.

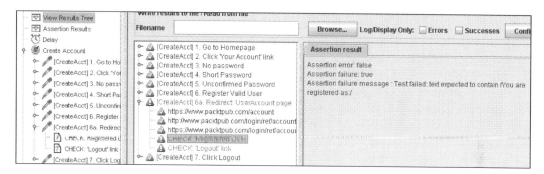

Summary

This chapter provided visual means for you to understand the capabilities of JMeter tools that support functional testing, as we directly wrote and implemented a JMeter script. We have demonstrated building a Test Plan to contain functional validations (or assertions) by incorporating various essential JMeter components, particularly the 'Response Assertion' element and 'Assertion Result' Listener. By using the 'User Defined Variable' Configuration element, we have also parameterized several values in order to give our Test Plan better flexibility. In addition, we have observed the result of these assertions as we performed a 'live' run of the application under test. An HTTP Request sampler may require to be modified, if there are any changes to the parameter(s) that the sampler sends with each request. Once created, a JMeter Test Plan that contains assertions can then be used and modified in subsequent Regression tests for the application. The next chapter will let us see various ways that a JMeter script can be further configured and tweaked so that it supports better portability and testability. Chapter 7 will describe various methods and tools available in JMeter that support more advanced and complex testing requirements.

7
Advanced Features

There are still more advanced features of JMeter than those we are familiar with. Chapter 5 and Chapter 6 have provided essential tools to build Test Plans that support Performance Testing and Functional Testing, respectively. This chapter will take us further into how we can enhance a basic Test Plan by using Regular Expressions and built-in Functions as supported by JMeter. This chapter will also introduce the Regular Expression Extractor, which I personally find very useful as it makes a Test Plan more practical than it is without the Extractor. Naturally, this chapter will give you a 'live' walkthrough of these features. In addition, since JMeter works on the protocol level, not only can we use it to test web applications, but also on many other Internet applications, such as FTP, LDAP, Databases, etc. Very little has been said about these other features, as web applications testing has been the dominant area of JMeter usage.

Although this chapter may not go into greater detail, it provides you with a more 'live' example on how these features can be used. We will use three Test Plans to demonstrate these features of JMeter: Web Test Plan, Database Test Plan, and FTP Test Plan. While 'Web Test Plan' tests a remote HTTP server, 'Database Test Plan' allow us to perform tests on a remote database server. Of course, 'FTP Test Plan' is used to perform tests on any remote File or FTP Server. The first section *Extending the Web Test Plan* will be based on a simple web application I have created for this book, while in the section *Testing a Database Server* will simply extract information from the same database that the web application is using, though using a different database schema. In *Testing an FTP server*, the FTP Test Plan will require a 'live' file server. For this chapter, we will use the localhost as the target 'web server', 'Database Server', and 'FTP Server'.

Extending the Web Test Plan

This section will help to give us more insight into how we can build a more robust, and flexible Web Test Plan. We will see how we can incorporate various features into a Test Plan, including Regular Expressions and Functions. To effectively demonstrate the use of these features, I have prepared beforehand a Functional Test Plan using a simple web application on the localhost as the target server. You can download this from the code bundle of Chapter 7 available on our website. The `volsys.rar` folder needs to be unzipped into the apps folder of the target application folder.

This simple application, Volsys, keeps contact information about its network of volunteers and maintains a schedule of work assignments for these volunteers. In brief, it allows the user to:

1. Log in to the application (the administrator is the only user, for now).

2. Add Volunteers—each registered volunteer will be assigned a unique volunteer ID.

3. Add Assignments—each registered assignment will be assigned a unique assignment ID and will be assigned to a volunteer.

4. Manage Assignments—the user can delete whole assignments or edit the details of an assignment.

5. Manage Volunteers—the user can delete volunteers from the repository or edit the details of a volunteer.

This chapter will demonstrate to you how these various feature can be used in at least one element of the Test Plan, and also the effects that they have on the test results.

Firstly, we will need to create five 'volunteers' in our list of volunteers. This application requires two pages to complete each add-new-volunteer transaction. The **Add Volunteer** page provides a GUI for the user to add and submit a new volunteer, while the **Most Recent Volunteer** page sends a registration confirmation and a Volunteer ID after every successful submission. This task will be quite daunting especially when we think about having to add a much longer list of volunteers (say 1000?) into the system via the browser.

On a different note, it is very tempting to use a **CSV Data Set Config** Configuration Element. However, there is a catch in using this element for this task. Once a csv file is opened, lines are read as the threads need them. Therefore, if we use this element to accomplish this task, we will need to simulate five user threads, which is unnecessary. This task only requires that a single thread or user should perform a similar set of tasks five times, using different variables each time. Using a **ForEach Controller** we can complete this task much faster. **While Controller** and **Loop Controller** are better alternatives to register a big number of volunteers.

Using the ForEach Controller

The **ForEach Controller** is used in tandem with **User Defined Variables (UDV)**. It is a variant of a **Loop Controller** as every sampler or controller that we add is executed one or more times according to the number of times to repeat. The difference is that it loops through the values of a set of related variables, where during each loop the variable has a new value. The set of input consists of multiple variables, each of which ends with a number. Note that the underscore is optional. Each input variable extension must have a specific value. The return (or output) variable will have the respective values as defined in the input values.

A sample **UDV-ForEach** pair looks as shown in the following snapshot:

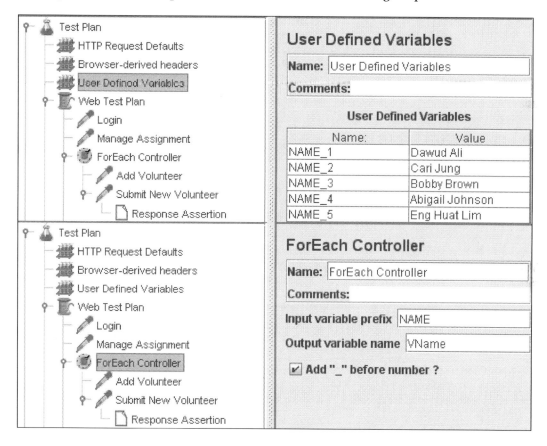

In this example, when the input variable has the name **NAME**, the following variables need to be defined as seen in the UDV element in the previous snapshot. Once the Controller is executed, it will loop five times, with each loop consisting of:

LOOP#	Input Variable	Input Variable Value	Output Variable	Output Variable Value
Loop 1	NAME_1	Dawud Ali	VName	Dawud Ali
Loop 2	NAME_2	Carl Jung	VName	Carl Jung
Loop 3	NAME_3	Bobby Brown	VName	Bobby Brown
Loop 4	NAME_4	Abigail Johnson	VName	Abigail Johnson
Loop 5	NAME_5	Eng Huat Lim	VName	Eng Huat Lim

The generated output variables can be used throughout the components contained within the **ForEach Controller**. You may need to add a simple assertion (see the following image) to ensure that the generated value is being used.

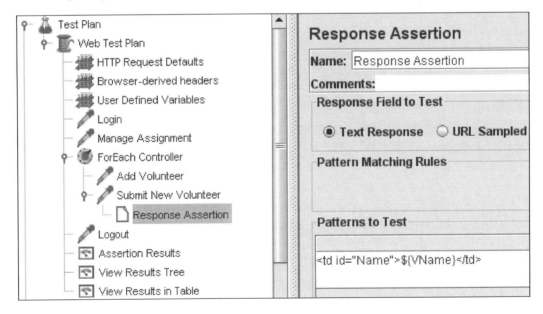

Using the While Controller and the StringFromFile Function

The **ForEach Controller** paired with the **User Defined Variable** element saves lot of time to run and execute a handful number of input variables, as long as they are entered in the UDV. However, there is an alternative to this method, where we can simply read a list of strings from an external text file. This method uses the **While Controller** and utilizes a predefined JMeter function, **__StringFromFile**. The While Controller will trigger the **__StringFromFile** function to open an external text file and read the file one string at a time, at each call of the function.

In this example, I have created `volunteer-list.txt` — a text-based file containing a list of volunteers' names — in the same path as the JMeter installation. The installation path is the default path for JMeter. You may place the file anywhere else in your machine, but you will need to define the exact path in the 'File Name' parameter of this function. In making use of the While Controller, `volunteer-list.txt` has the string **false** as the last entry. Upon reading the string 'false' from the file, the loop will exit. The second parameter of this function should be the name of a variable that will contain the value currently being read from the text file. The samplers that follow can use the value in this variable to proceed with the next tasks. The following snapshot illustrates both elements for this example.

During iteration of this while loop, the function **__StringFromFile** reads each line from the file `volunteer-list.txt` and assigns each read value to the variable `VName`.

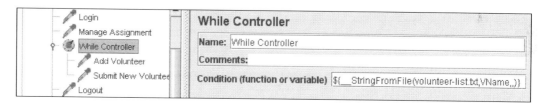

The following snapshot demonstrates that, in each iteration, the read value assigned to variable VName is later used as a value for the parameter volunteer_name in the **Submit New Volunteer** sampler.

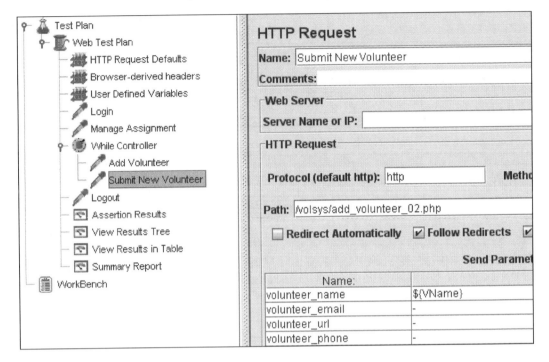

Using the Loop Controller and the StringFromFile Function

Similar to the 'While Controller' is the **Loop Controller**, except that we will need to determine how many times its child elements need to repeat. Notice also that the **Submit New Volunteer** element reads each string from the file using the __StringFromFile function. The file is opened once and remains opened as long as the loop continues. This function will read the string one line at a time and reads a new line at each loop. The following snapshot demonstrates the Controller-Sampler pair for this task.

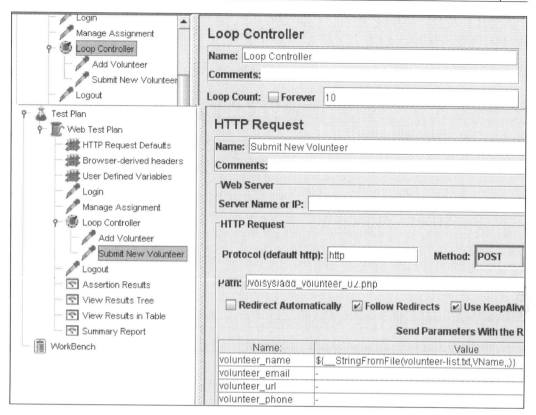

Whichever method you may choose to use, it will certainly perform repeated tasks within a fraction of time as compared to the time you will require to do it manually. **Save** and **Run** the test to create at least five volunteers for the use of the next tasks.

Using Regular Expressions

Wikipedia, the online Encyclopedia describes regular expression as:

> ... *provide a concise and flexible means for identifying strings of text of interest, such as particular characters, words, or patterns of characters. Regular expressions ... are written in a formal language that can be interpreted by a regular expression processor, a program that either serves as a parser generator or examines text and identifies parts that match the provided specification.*

Regular expressions are used to search and manipulate text, based on patterns. JMeter interprets forms of regular expressions or patterns being used throughout a JMeter test plan, by including the pattern matching software Apache Jakarta ORO. You may visit its URL: `http://jakarta.apache.org/oro` for more information on regular expression patterns and rules. The API for package `org.apache.oro.text.regex` gives you a summary of regular expressions patterns. With the use of regular expressions, we can certainly save a lot of time and achieve greater flexibility as we create or enhance a Test Plan.

You can place regular expressions in any component in a Test Plan. The next step will demonstrate the use of Regular expressions in the Regular Expression Extractor—a Post-Processor Element. This element will extract text from the current page using a Regular Expression to identify the text pattern that a desired element conforms with.

Note that as we added each volunteer, we did not record the IDs that are automatically generated by the application. Instead, we will do this after all volunteers have been added. Therefore, our next step is to view the volunteer list and later edit one of these volunteers. We will select the volunteer in the second row of the volunteer table seen in the **Manage Volunteer** page. The next step is to edit and update information, using the volunteer's ID. Note that this table is sorted by the volunteer name, not the volunteer ID.

To capture the ID of this volunteer, let us first determine the pattern where we will find the volunteer in the second row. As can be seen in the following snapshot, the ID of the second volunteer is surrounded by `<td id="ID">` and `</td >`, and it is the second row of data having this pattern. We can use this to match the exact pattern that we want to extract information from. As we want to extract two pieces of information from this page, the volunteer ID and the volunteer's name, the fields are defined as follows:

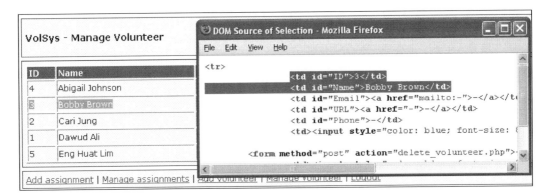

The **Regular Expression** field in the following snapshot encapsulates the highlighted text in the previous image. All fields will be explained in the table that follows.

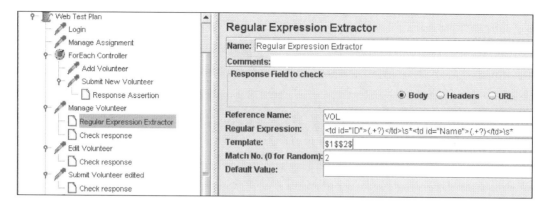

The **Regular Expression Extractor** control panel as shown in the previous snapshot defines these fields as follows:

Field	Explanation
Reference Name	The name of the variable in which the extracted test will be stored (refname).
Regular Expression	The pattern against which the text to be extracted will be matched. The text groups that will extracted are enclosed by the characters '(' and ')'. We use '.+?' to indicate a single instance of the text enclosed by the `<td..>...</td>` tags.
Template	Each group of text extracted will be placed as a member of the variable VOL, following the order of each group of pattern enclosed by '(' and ')'. Each group is stored as `refname_g#`, where refname is the string you entered as the reference name, and # is the group number. **1** to refers to group 1, **2** to refers to group 2, etc. **0** refers to whatever the entire expression matches. In this example, the ID we extract will be maintained in `VOL_g1`, while the Name value will be stored in `VOL_g2`.
Match No.	Since we plan to extract only the second occurrence of this pattern, matching the second volunteer, we use value 2. Value 0 would make a random matching, while a negative value needs to be used with the ForEach Controller.
Default	If the item is not found, this will be the default value. This is an optional field. You may leave it blank.

After extracting the ID of the record that we want to edit, we are ready to select, edit, and update this record.

The following HTTP Sampler selects the volunteer record having volunteer_id=3 for editing.

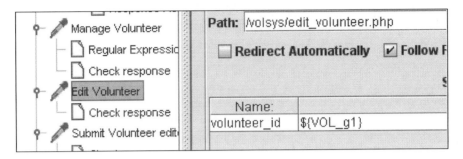

The following HTTP Sampler modifies the selected volunteer record (volunteer_id=3). It modifies the record fields email, URL, and phone from values '-' (refer to the Controller-Sampler snapshot shown earlier in the chapter) to the new values seen in the following snapshot.

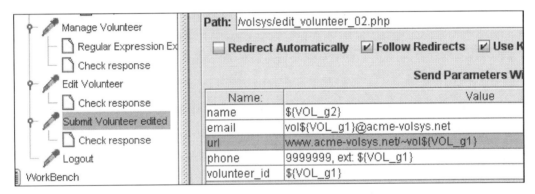

We may want to assert that these values were correctly updated by means of a Response Assertion in the 'Manage Volunteer' page that follows. To ensure that the data is updated correctly, the assertion may verify the following pattern:

```
<td id="ID">${VOL_g1}</td>\s*<td id="Name">${VOL_g2}</td>\s*
<td id="Email"><a href="mailto:vol${VOL_g1}@acme-volsys.net">
   vol${VOL_g1}@acme-volsys.net</a></td>\s*
<td id="URL"><a href="www.acme-volsys.net/~vol${VOL_g1}">
   www.acme-volsys.net/~vol${VOL_g1}</a></td>\s*
<td id="Phone">9999999, ext: ${VOL_g1}</td>
```

Note that Regular Expressions are used in the entire assertion above. Please refer to the Jakarta ORO URL to know more about the regular expressions patterns that JMeter is able to evaluate.

To complete this section of the chapter, add a few Listeners to capture the result of this Test Plan. **Save** the Test Plan and **Run**. You are free to experiment with these advanced features of JMeter in other pages of the application.

The next two sections of this chapter are different sort of testing using JMeter than you have been familiar with.

Testing a Database Server

A few things you will need before proceeding to build a Database Test Plan are:

1. A working database driver. Following the database that you are using on your database server, copy the `.jar` file contained in the database driver and paste it in the `lib` folder of your JMeter installation path.

2. A valid database-schema.

3. Valid non-empty database table(s).

4. A valid user-level access to the database. It is important for the database to have a user other than the root user for testing purpose, in order to prevent any potential data misuse.

For this section I have set up a simple database, MySQL, being localhost as the Database Server. I have also prepared a database schema—"world". This schema (free for non-commercial use) can be downloaded from the MySQL home site: `http://dev.mysql.com/doc/`. On this site go to section "Example Database", find world database, download db and either gzip it or zip it. The username for this exercise will be **guest**, while the password is also **guest**. This section will demonstrate multiple requests to execute an SQL statement directed to a Database Server.

As usual we will start off by adding a thread group to the Test Plan. You may need to configure in order to have 1000 threads, with minimal start-up time, e.g. 3 seconds, with multiple repeats—just to demonstrate how far we can test a database in this manner. Then, add a **JDBC Connection Configuration** as the thread's first child. You may choose to use the default values or configure as you wish in tandem with the database in use. For this Test Plan, configure as following:

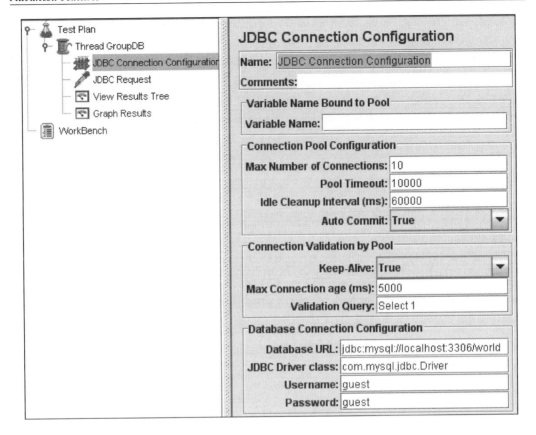

Add a **JDBC Request** sampler to the thread, and create an SQL statement that serves your testing purpose. I used a simple SQL query for this example.

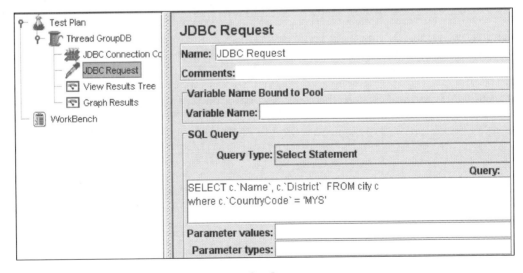

You may want to add assertions to the sampler to verify that it returns the expected results. **Save** and **Run** the Test Plan as needed.

While this example serves a simple 'live' Database Test Plan, you may want to visit `http://jakarta.apache.org/jmeter/usermanual/build-db-test-plan.html` and the JMeter user manual to learn more about setting up a Database Test Plan.

Testing an FTP Server

Finally for this *Testing an FTP Server* section, I have set up the localhost as the target File Server, and the file paths to demonstrate the use of FTP Samplers.

What you will need before proceeding to build a FTP Test Plan includes:

1. A running FTP server on the target machine.
2. A valid path to the shared files in your FTP server.
3. Valid non-empty files in the FTP installation path.
4. A valid user-level access to the files.

For this section I have set up a simple FTP Server—Gold FTP Server, running on localhost. I have also prepared a simple text file—`test.txt` in the Shared Folder of this FTP Server. It simply contains the string "This is a test". The username for this exercise will be **anonymous**, while the default password is **mozilla@test.com**. This section will demonstrate multiple requests for files directed to a file server.

As usual we will start off by adding a Thread Group to the Test Plan. You may need to configure in order to have multiple threads, with minimal start-up time, with multiple repeats—just to demonstrate how far we can test a file server in this manner. Then, add an **FTP Request Defaults** element as the thread's first child. You may choose to use the default values or configure as you wish in tandem with the file server in use. Add an FTP Request sampler to the thread, and configure as seen in the following snapshot:

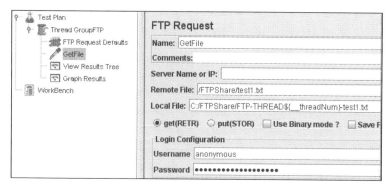

Note that this sampler requests a file located in the FTP Share folder of the file server, downloads it and saves it using a different file name in the download path. The downloaded file names are created following the thread number generated by each thread that makes the file request. This effect is achieved by appending the __threadNum__ function—a JMETER built-in function—to the thread's own copy of the downloaded file.

For example, if you have set the number of Threads to 3, following the configuration above, at the end of the Test Plan, you will find filenames: `FTP-THREAD1-test1.txt`, `FTP-THREAD2-test1.txt`, and `FTP-THREAD3-test1.txt`. The number after the word 'THREAD' was appended as a result of calling the __threadNum__ function.

You may want to add assertions to the sampler to verify that it returns the expected results. **Save** and **Run** the Test Plan as needed.

This example provides you with a simple 'live' FTP Test Plan; you may want to visit (`http://jakarta.apache.org/jmeter/usermanual/build-ftp-test-plan.html`) and the JMeter User Manual to learn more about setting up an FTP Test Plan.

Summary

JMeter provides a variety of tools, elements, and functionalities to let the tester create a highly modifiable, robust, and extensible Test Plan. Assertions, regular expressions, and built-in functions certainly add more functionality to your Test Plan. What is more interesting is that, unlike many other testing tools, JMeter can test a wide range of Internet applications, and is not limited to web applications only. While this chapter has demonstrated testing on Web Server, Database Server and File/FTP Server, there are more than a dozen Request samplers in JMeter that you can use to test various applications, making your JMeter Test Plan very scalable. Moreover, with over 15 Controllers and over 20 built-in functions, you can make your Test Plan even more robust. There is much more that JMeter can do than what we have gone through in Chapter 5 through Chapter 7. The JMeter user manual (`http://jakarta.apache.org/jmeter/usermanual`) can tell all; however, it may take lots of practice and time to effectively digest the manual. This is just an introductory book that introduces us to a powerful testing tool—JMeter.

8

JMeter and Beyond

This book does not tell you everything about JMeter. So far we have simply set the path for more discoveries about JMeter. This book gives the beginner a head start, maybe even a clean start on JMeter and test automation in general. The JMeter online manual and the project forum may give you more details in a more technical manner. Subsequently, how then would this book be helpful? Upon completing this tiny book, you will find that it tries to simplify the learning process for a beginner trying to set his or her first heels in automation, or specifically, in JMeter. It should give you a quick and clear idea about JMeter and similar tools that can help you in a testing project.

For a test engineer, looking for an alternative to manually perform regression testing or looking for quick solutions to perform load testing, this book may provide an almost complete overview of this tool.

For a test Manager, or test Lead doing research on the cost-effective testing tools that the team or organization can afford to have, JMeter may just be one of those tools to start with.

I hope that this book will be a boon to get your feet wet on this tool. Up to the date this text is written, there is no other book like it so far. Other books may talk about JMeter, but sadly enough, only very briefly; merely as a chapter or part of a chapter. Other vendor-centric testing tools may have just as rich or richer sets of features as JMeter, but they can cost up to five-figures of the organization's budget, and of course with limited licenses. On the other hand, you can get JMeter on a free, open-source license. However, like any other open-source tools, there isn't really a vendor available for support. However, if the organization can lend some time for the test engineer to learn this tool, that is probably all the investment you will need to benefit from this tool. Besides that, on days when you need to generate tests more than a single machine can handle, you may want to perform a distributed testing (see `http://jakarta.apache.org/jmeter/usermanual/remote-test.html`), run JMeter in non-GUI mode (`http://jakarta.apache.org/jmeter/usermanual/best-practices.html`), or invest in some higher-end machine to run your tests.

Once you have covered the basics this book has presented, you may wish to discover more of JMeter from its online manual—http://jakarta.apache.org/jmeter/usermanual/index.html. Just to briefly describe a few items, the 'HTTP URL Re-writing Modifier' and the 'Cookie Manager' are normally included in the Test Plan if your web application maintains a certain state for each user, e.g. cookies, URL re-writing. You may need to use the Authorization Manager element at times when you need to have direct access to the server, if, for example, you want to monitor web server, it lets you specify user logins for pages that are restricted using server authentication. Another feature that you might be interested to know more about is remote (or distributed) testing, a feature that JMeter provides in support of stress testing. This remote testing has been mentioned only briefly in Chapter 5, in the section *Remote Testing with JMeter*. JMeter even supports a remote server monitoring tool to measure its performance by incorporating the Authorization Manager element and Monitor Listener in your JMeter Remote Testing.

Additionally, if you can program in Java, you may extend JMeter by building add-ons, which does not require that you build (or compile) JMeter. On the other hand, if instead you want to add more components or modify an existing component in the JMeter API, you may simply build JMeter using Ant. For more information on building JMeter and add-ons, visit http://jakarta.apache.org/jmeter/building.html.

If you need to simulate random behavior in a Test Plan, Random Controller and Random Order Controllers may be of particular interest to you. These are normally used when the Test Plan performs more than one pass through a group of child elements. The effect of Random Controller is similar to that of Interleave Controller except that instead of going in sequential order through its child elements, it picks and executes one at random at each pass. Random Order Controller will execute each child element at most once, but the order of execution of the nodes will be random. Include Controller allows you to incorporate external .jmx files if you are not comfortable in merging into the current Test Plan, which would only increase its complexity and size.

There are dozens more JMeter components that this tiny book has not covered. To have all these in a single book while keeping to the same simple approach for the readers would turn out too overwhelming. We might end up with a few more volumes. This book simply gives a practical, no-nonsense first look at JMeter, as it paves way for the reader to learn more about this great tool from its online manual, the project forums, and the Internet.

What this book has covered so far would help give the reader a first impression of JMeter. Following is a quick list (adapted from the online-manual) of the Components in JMeter that we have covered (checkmarked) and those that we didn't:

Samplers	Listeners	Assertions	Timers
Samplers tell JMeter to send a request to a server and wait for a response. Following is the list of JMeter Samplers:	Provide access to the information JMeter gathers about the test cases while JMeter runs. Following is list of JMeter Listners:	Allow you to assert facts about responses received from the server being tested. Following is the list of JMeter Assertions:	Cause JMeter to pause for a certain amount of time before each request a thread group makes. Following is the list of Timers:
☑ FTP Request	☑ Sample Result Save Configuration	☑ Response Assertion	☑ Constant Timer
☑ HTTP Request	☑ Graph Full Results	☐ Duration Assertion	☐ Gaussian Random Timer
☑ JDBC Request	☑ Graph Results	☐ Size Assertion	☐ Uniform Random Timer
☐ Java Request	☐ Spline Visualizer	☐ XML Assertion	☐ Constant Throughput Timer
☐ SOAP/XML-RPC Request		☐ BeanShell Assertion	☐ Synchronizing Timer
☐ WebService (SOAP) Request	☑ Assertion Results	☐ MD5Hex Assertion	
	☑ View Results Tree		☐ BeanShell Timer
☐ LDAP Request	☑ Aggregate Report	☐ HTML Assertion	
☐ LDAP Extended Request	☑ View Results in Table	☐ XPath Assertion	
☐ Access Log Sampler	☐ Simple Data Writer	☐ XML Schema Assertion	
☐ BeanShell Sampler	☐ Monitor Results		
☐ BSF Sampler	☐ Distribution Graph (alpha)		
☐ TCP Sampler	☐ Aggregate Graph		
☐ JMS Publisher	☐ Mailer Visualizer		
☐ JMS Subscriber	☐ BeanShell Listener		
☐ JMS Point-to-Point	☑ Summary Report		
☐ JUnit Request			
☐ Mail Reader Sampler			
☐ Test Action			

Logic Controllers	Configuration Elements	Pre-Processors
Let you customize the logic that JMeter uses to decide when to send requests. Following is the list of JMeter Logic controllers:	These are used to add or modify requests made by Samplers. Following is the list of configuration elements:	Modify the settings of a Sample Request just before it runs, or to update variables that are not extracted from response text. Following is the list of Pre-Processors elements:
☑ Simple Controller	☑ CSV Data Set Config	☐ HTML Link Parser
	☑ FTP Request Defaults	☐ HTTP URL Re-writing Modifier
☑ Loop Controller		
☐ Once Only Controller	HTTP Authorization Manager	☐ HTML Parameter Mask
		☐ HTTP User Parameter Modifier
☐ Interleave Controller	HTTP Cookie Manager	
☐ Random Controller	☑ HTTP Request Defaults	☑ User Parameters
☐ Random Order Controller	☑ HTTP Header Manager	☐ Counter
☐ Throughput Controller	Java Request Defaults	☐ BeanShell PreProcessor
☐ Runtime Controller	☑ JDBC Connection Configuration	
☐ If Controller	Login Config Element	
☑ While Controller	LDAP Request Defaults	
☐ Switch Controller	LDAP Extended Request Defaults	
☑ ForEach Controller	TCP Sampler Config	
☐ Module Controller	☑ User Defined Variables	
☐ Include Controller	☐ Simple Config Element	
☐ Transaction Controller		
☑ Recording Controller		

Post-Processors	Functions and Variables		Miscellaneous Features
Post-processors execute after a request has been made from a Sampler. They are often used to process the response data. Following is the list of Post-Processors elements:	JMeter functions are special values that can populate fields of any Sampler or other element in a test tree. Variables are local to a thread. Following is the list of Functions and Variables:		Following is the list of miscellaneous features of JMeter:
☑ Regular Expression Extractor	☐ regexFunction	☐ setProperty	☑ Test Plan
☐ XPath Extractor	☑ counter	☐ log	☑ Thread Group
☐ Result Status Action Handler	☑ threadNum	☐ logn	☑ WorkBench
☐ Save Responses to a file	☐ intSum	☐ BeanShell	☐ SSL Manager
☐ Generate Summary Results	☑ StringFromFile	☐ split	☑ HTTP Proxy Server
☐ BeanShell PostProcessor	☐ machineName	☐ XPath	☐ HTTP Mirror Server
	☐ javaScript	☐ time	☐ Property Display
	☐ Random	☐ jexl	☐ Debug Sampler
	☐ CSVRead	☐ V	☐ Debug PostProcessor
	☐ property	☐ eval	
	☐ P	☐ evalVar	

Summary

This chapter discusses briefly on what more JMeter has and can do for its users. It tells the reader where to go in order to find more information about other elements of JMeter that this book does not have.

At the beginning part of the book, we discussed a number of concerns regarding test automation, and how automation suits your testing needs. In later chapters, we gradually moved from briefly overviewing JMeter to creating functional and performance Test Plans that work. Furthermore, in Chapter 7, we learned to use a number of auxiliary features of JMeter that are useful to make Test Plans more flexible and robust. A brief description of all components of JMeter is available in Appendix A.

There is more work in the pipeline for the JMeter project about which you can learn more in the project's WIKI pages, `http://wiki.apache.org/jakarta-jmeter`. If you are skilled in Java, you may customize the JMeter API, build your own add-ons, or may even consider being a code contributor to the JMeter project. The project's mailing list would be another important resource both to JMeter users (`http://mail-archives.apache.org/mod_mbox/jakarta-jmeter-user`) and JMeter developers (`http://mail-archives.apache.org/mod_mbox/jakarta-jmeter-dev`).

A
Component Description

Following is a table briefly explaining the components mentioned in this book. The description is adapted from the JMeter online manual. For more detailed information about these components, visit http://jakarta.apache.org/jmeter/usermanual.

Samplers	
FTP Request	Lets you send an FTP "retrieve file" or "upload file" request to an FTP server. When downloading a file, it can be stored on disk (Local File) or in the Response Data, or both.
HTTP Request	Lets you send an HTTP/HTTPS request to a web server. It also lets you control whether or not JMeter parses HTML files for images and other embedded resources and sends HTTP/HTTPS requests to retrieve them.
JDBC Request	Lets you send an SQL query to a database.
Java Request	Lets you control a Java class that implements the JavaSamplerClient interface. By writing your own implementation of this interface, you can use JMeter to harness multiple threads, input parameter control, and data collection.
SOAP/XML-RPC Request	Lets you send a SOAP request to a Web Service. It can also be used to send XML-RPC over HTTP.
WebService (SOAP) Request	Uses Apache SOAP driver to serialize the message and set the header with the correct SOAP action.
LDAP Request	Lets you send one of four LDAP requests (Add, Modify, Delete, and Search) to an LDAP server.
LDAP Extended Request	Can send all 8 different LDAP requests to an LDAP server. It is an extended version of the LDAP sampler, therefore it is harder to configure, but can be used to make a test much more closely resembling a real LDAP session.

Samplers

Access Log Sampler	Designed to read access logs and generate HTTP requests.
BeanShell Sampler	Allows the user to write a Sampler using the BeanShell scripting language.
BSF Sampler	Allows you to write a sampler using a BSF scripting language. See the Apache Bean Scripting Framework website for details of the languages supported.
TCP Sampler	Opens a TCP/IP connection to the specified server. It then sends the text, and waits for a response.
JMS Publisher	Publishes messages to a given pub/sub topic. For those not familiar with JMS, it is the J2EE specification for messaging.
JMS Subscriber	Subscribes to messages in a given pub/sub topic. For those not familiar with JMS, it is the J2EE specification for messaging.
JMS Point-to-Point	This sampler sends and optionally receives JMS Messages through point-to-point connections (queues). This is different from pub/sub messages and is generally used for handling transactions.
JUnit Request	The current implementation supports standard JUnit convention and extensions. It also includes extensions like oneTimeSetUp and oneTimeTearDown.
Mail Reader Sampler	Not yet implemented. TBA.
Test Action	This sampler is intended for use in a conditional controller. Rather than generate a sample, the test element either pauses or stops the selected target.

Logic Controllers

Simple Controller	Lets you organize your Samplers and other Logic Controllers. This controller provides no functionality beyond that of a storage device.
Loop Controller	Lets JMeter to loop through its child controllers a certain number of times, in addition to the loop value you specified for the Thread Group.
Once Only Controller	It tells JMeter to process the controller(s) inside it only once, and pass over any requests under it during further iterations through the Test Plan.
Interleave Controller	Lets JMeter to alternate among the controllers for each loop iteration.
Random Controller	Acts similarly to the Interleave Controller, except that instead of going in order through its sub-controllers and samplers, it picks one randomly at each pass.
Random Order Controller	Much like a Simple Controller, it will execute each child element at most once, but the order of execution of the nodes will be random.
Throughput Controller	Allows the user to control how often it is executed.
Runtime Controller	Controls the time for which its children are allowed to run.

Logic Controllers

If Controller	Allows the user to control whether the test elements below it (its children) are run or not.
While Controller	Runs its children until the condition is "false".
Switch Controller	Acts like the Interleave Controller in that it runs one of the subordinate elements on each iteration but rather than run them in sequence, the controller runs the element number defined by the switch value. If the switch value is out of range, it will run the zeroth element, which therefore acts as default.
ForEach Controller	This controller loops through the values of a set of related variables. When you add samplers (or controllers) to a ForEach Controller, every sample Sampler (or controller) is executed one or more times, where during every loop the variable has a new value.
Module Controller	Provides a mechanism for substituting Test Plan fragments into the current Test Plan at run time.
Include Controller	Designed to use an external jmx file. To use it, add samples to a Simple Controller, then save the Simple Controller as a .jmx file. The file can then be used in a Test Plan. However, this element does not support variables/functions in the filename field, but can be overridden if the property includecontroller.prefix is defined where the contents are used to prefix the pathname.
Transaction Controller	Used to group Samplers by generating an additional sample, which totals the nested samplers.
Recording Controller	Simply a place-holder indicating where the proxy server should record samples to. It has no effect during a test run. But during recording using the HTTP Proxy Server, all recorded samples will by default be saved under the Recording Controller.

Listeners

Sample Result Save Configuration	Listeners can be configured to save different items to the result log files (JTL) by using the Config popup as shown below. The defaults are defined as described in the Listener Default Configuration documentation. Items with (CSV) only apply to the CSV format; items with (XML) only apply to XML format. CSV format cannot be used to save any items that include line-breaks.
Graph Full Results	Not implemented yet. TBA.
Graph Results	Generates a simple graph that plots all sample times. Along the bottom of the graph, the current sample (black), the current average of all samples (blue), the current standard deviation (red), and the current throughput rate (green) are displayed in milliseconds.
Spline Visualizer	Provides a view of all sample times from the start of the test till the end, regardless of how many samples have been taken.
Assertion Results	This visualizer shows the Label of each sample taken. It also reports failures of any Assertions that are part of the Test Plan.

Listeners

View Results Tree	This shows a tree of all sample responses, allowing you to view the response for any sample. In addition to showing the response, you can see the time it took to get this response, and some response codes. There are several ways to view the response, selectable by a radio button.
Aggregate Report	The aggregate report creates a table row for each differently named request in your test. For each request, it totals the response information and provides request count, Min, Max, Average, Error %, Throughput (request/second), and KB/second throughput.
View Results in Table	This visualizer creates a row for every sample result. Like the View Results Tree, it uses a lot of memory.
Simple Data Writer	This listener can record results to a file but not to the UI. It is meant to provide an efficient means of recording data by eliminating GUI overhead.
Monitor Results	Visualizer for displaying server status. It is designed for Tomcat 5, but any servlet container can port the status servlet and use this monitor.
Distribution Graph	This will display a bar for every unique response time.
Aggregate Graph	Similar to the Aggregate Report, the difference is the aggregate graph provides an easy way to generate bar graphs and save the graph as a PNG file.
Mailer Visualizer	The mailer visualizer can be set up to send email if a test run receives too many failed responses from the server.
BeanShell Listener	The BeanShell Listener allows the use of BeanShell for processing samples for saving, etc. The BeanShell `jar` file is not included with JMeter; it needs to be separately downloaded. Please see the BeanShell website at `http://www.beanshell.org`.
Summary Report	This report creates a table row for each differently named request in your test. This is similar to the Aggregate Report, except that it uses less memory.

Configuration Elements

CSV Data Set Config	Used to read lines from a file, and split them into variables. Easier to use than the `__CSVRead()` and `_StringFromFile()` functions, the file is only opened once, and each thread will use a different line from the file. Lines are read as the threads need them.
FTP Request Defaults	No documentation found.
HTTP Authorization Manager	Lets you specify one or more user logins for web pages that are restricted using server authentication.

Configuration Elements

HTTP Cookie Manager	This stores and sends cookies just like a web browser. If you are testing a website that uses a cookie for storing session information, each JMeter thread will have its own session. You can manually add a cookie to the Cookie Manager. However, if you do this, the cookie will be shared by all JMeter threads.
HTTP Request Defaults	Lets you set default values that your HTTP Request controllers use.
HTTP Header Manager	Lets you add or override HTTP request headers.
Java Request Defaults	Lets you set default values for Java testing. See the Java Request.
JDBC Connection Configuration	Creates a database connection pool (used by JDBC Request Sampler) with JDBC Connection settings.
Login Config Element	Lets you add or override username and password settings in samplers that use username and password as part of their setup.
LDAP Request Defaults	Lets you set default values for LDAP testing. See the LDAP Request.
LDAP Extended Request Defaults	Lets you set default values for extended LDAP testing.
TCP Sampler Config	Provides default data for the TCP Sampler.
User Defined Variables	Lets you define variables for use in other test elements, just as in the Test Plan. The variables in User Defined Variables components will take precedence over those defined closer to the tree root—including those defined in the Test Plan.
Simple Config Element	Lets you add or override arbitrary values in Samplers. You can choose the name of the value and the value itself.

Assertions

Response Assertion	Lets you add pattern strings to be compared against various fields of the response. The pattern strings are Perl5-style Regular Expressions.
Duration Assertion	This tests that each response was received within a given amount of time. Any response that takes longer than the given number is marked as a failed response.
Size Assertion	This tests that each response contains the right number of bytes in it. You can specify that the size be equal to, greater than, less than, or not equal to a given number of bytes.
XML Assertion	This tests that the response data consists of a formally correct XML document. It does not validate the XML based on a DTD or schema or do any further validation.
BeanShell Assertion	Allows the user to perform assertion checking using a BeanShell script.
MD5Hex Assertion	Allows the user to check the MD5 hash of the response data.

Assertions

HTML Assertion	Allows the user to check the HTML syntax of the response data using JTidy.
XPath Assertion	The XPath Assertion tests a document for well formedness and has the option of validating against a DTD, or putting the document through JTidy and testing for an XPath.
XML Schema Assertion	The XML Schema Assertion allows the user to validate a response against an XML Schema.

Timers

Constant Timer	Allows each thread to pause for the same amount of time between requests.
Gaussian Random Timer	Pauses each thread request for a random amount of time, with most of the time intervals occurring near a particular value. The total delay is the sum of the Gaussian distributed value (with mean 0.0 and standard deviation 1.0) times the deviation value you specify, and the offset value.
Uniform Random Timer	Pauses each thread request for a random amount of time, with each time interval having the same probability of occurring. The total delay is the sum of the random value and the offset value.
Constant Throughput Timer	Allows for variable pauses, calculated to keep the total throughput (in terms of samples per minute) as close as possible to a give figure.
Synchronizing Timer	Blocks threads until X number of threads have been blocked, and then releases them all at once. It can thus create large instant loads at various points of the Test Plan.
BeanShell Timer	The BeanShell Timer can be used to generate a delay.

Pre-Processors

HTML Link Parser	Parses HTML response from the server and extracts links and forms.
HTTP URL Re-writing Modifier	This modifier works similarly to the HTML Link Parser, but is especially useful for web applications that use URL Re-writing to store session IDs instead of cookies.
HTML Parameter Mask	This element is deprecated. Use Counter instead of this parameter. The HTML Parameter Mask is used to generate unique values for HTML arguments.
HTTP User Parameter Modifier	This element is deprecated. Use User Parameters instead of this parameter. The User Parameter Modifier uses an XML file get values for HTTP arguments. Any HTTP Request that this modifier modifies will be checked for the existence of the specified arguments.

Pre-Processors

User Parameters	Allows the user to specify values for User Variables specific to individual threads, which can be accessed in any test component in the same thread group, using the function syntax: `${variable}`.
Counter	Allows the user to create a counter that can be referenced anywhere in the Thread Group. The counter now uses long to store the value, so the range is from -2^63 to 2^63-1.
BeanShell PreProcessor	Allows arbitrary code to be applied before taking a sample.

Post-Processors

Regular Expression Extractor	Allows the user to extract values from a server response using a Perl-type regular expression. This element will execute after each Sample request in its scope, apply the regular expression extracting the requested values, generate the template string, and store the result into the given variable.
XPath Extractor	Allows the user to extract values from a structured response — XML or (X)HTML — using XPath query language.
Result Status Action Handler	Allows the user to stop the thread or the whole test if the relevant sampler failed.
Save Responses to a file	For each sample in its scope, it will create a file of the response Data. The primary use for this is in creating functional tests.
Generate Summary Results	Generates a summary of the test run so far to the log file and/or standard output. Both running and differential totals are shown.
BeanShell PostProcessor	Allows arbitrary code to be applied after taking a sample.

Miscellaneous Features

Test Plan	The Test Plan is where the overall settings for a test are specified.
Thread Group	A Thread Group defines a pool of users that will execute a particular test case against your server. You can control the number of users simulated (num of threads), the ramp up time (how long it takes to start all the threads), the number of times to perform the test, and optionally, a start and stop time for the test.
WorkBench	The WorkBench simply provides a place to temporarily store test elements while not in use, for copy/paste purposes, or any other purpose you desire.
SSL Manager	The SSL Manager is a way to select a client certificate so that you can test applications that use **Public Key Infrastructure (PKI)**. It is only needed if you have not set up the appropriate System properties.

Miscellaneous Features

HTTP Proxy Server	The Proxy Server can only record HTTP traffic. It is not possible to record HTTPS (SSL) sessions; however, there is an HTTPS spoofing mode to override this.
HTTP Mirror Server	This simply mirrors the data sent to it. This is useful for checking the content of HTTP Requests.
Property Display	Shows the values of System or JMeter properties. Values can be changed by entering new text in the Value column. It is available only on the WorkBench.
Debug Sampler	Generates a sample containing the values of all JMeter variables and/or properties. The values can be seen in the View Results Tree Listener Response Data pane.
Debug PostProcessor	Creates a subsample with the details of the previous sampler properties. This is intended for developer use only.

Functions and Variables

regexFunction	Parse previous response using a Regular Expression
counter	Generate an incrementing number
threadNum	Get thread number
intSum	Add numbers
StringFromFile	Read a line from a file
machineName	Get the local machine name
javaScript	Process JavaScript (Mozilla Rhino)
Random	Generate a random number
CSVRead	Read from a CSV delimited file
property	Read a property
P	Read a property (shorthand method)
setProperty	Set a JMeter property
log	Log (or display) a message (and return the value)
logn	Log (or display) a message (empty return value)
BeanShell	Run a BeanShell script
split	Split a string into variables
XPath	Use an XPath expression to read from a file
time	Return current time in various formats
jexl	Evaluate a Commons JEXL expression
V	Evaluate a variable name
eval	Evaluate a variable expression
evalVar	Evaluate an expression stored in a variable

Resources

Useful References

`http://jakarta.apache.org/jmeter`

Official JMeter Jakarta project website. This site offers links for the latest JMeter downloads, documentation, tutorials, and community:

`http://jakarta.apache.org/jmeter/usermanual/index.html`

The official online JMeter User manual. This site provides a detailed and more technical description of JMeter components and how to use them:

`http://wiki.apache.org/jakarta-jmeter`

These JMeter Wiki pages may be accessed to read, contribute, or modify content. They contain information and external links by contributors/users of JMeter, including FAQs and links that are directly or indirectly related to JMeter and Software Testing:

`http://mail-archives.apache.org/mod_mbox/jakarta-jmeter-user`
Archived mailing lists for JMeter users, dating from Mar 2001 until the most recent entry.

`http://mail-archives.apache.org/mod_mbox/jakarta-jmeter-dev`
Archived mailing lists for JMeter developers, dating from Feb 2001 until the most recent entry.

`http://www.opensourcetesting.org`
This site provides users with a wealth of information about open-source testing tools that are available.

`http://video.google.com`
Search this site with keyword "jmeter". Features online videos that serve as a guide for using JMeter.

`http://www.stpmag.com/issues/stp-2007-11.pdf`
Downloadable PDF version of "Software Test & Performance" magazine. Discusses JMeter pairing with Selenium to optimize Web-based testing.

Weblogs/Articles on Experience of Using JMeter

`http://weblogs.java.net/blog/johnreynolds/archive/2003/12/adventures_with.html`
This site talks about a user's first experience using JMeter.

`http://themindstorms.wordpress.com/2007/01/10/groovy-support-for-jmeter`
This site briefly talks about how Groovy 1.0 can integrate with JMeter for monitoring script.

`http://themindstorms.wordpress.com/2007/01/10/groovy-support-for-jmeter`
Another satisfied user's blog.

`http://www.ibm.com/developerworks/opensource/library/os-jmeter/_`
IBM IT Architect Greg Herringer's (`gherring@ca.ibm.com`) experience using JMeter for performance testing: "Test WebSphere performance with Apache JMeter: An open source tool, ideal for testing IFX messaging middleware".

Glossary

The terms which appear in the following appendix are adapted from "Standard glossary of terms used in Software Testing", Version 2.0 (dd. December, 2nd 2007), Produced by the 'Glossary Working Party' — International Software Testing Qualifications Board. Only those terms related to test automation are included here.

actual result: The behavior produced/observed when a component or system is tested.

ad hoc testing: Testing carried out informally; no formal test preparation takes place, no recognized test design technique is used, there are no expectations for results and arbitrariness guides the test execution activity.

automated testware: Testware used in automated testing, such as tool scripts.

availability: The degree to which a component or system is operational and accessible when required for use. Often expressed as a percentage.

basis test set: A set of test cases derived from the internal structure of a component or specification to ensure that 100% of a specified coverage criterion will be achieved.

behavior: The response of a component or system to a set of input values and preconditions.

benchmark test: (1) A standard against which measurements or comparisons can be made. (2) A test that is being used to compare components or systems to each other or to a standard as in (1).

boundary value: An input value or output value that is on the edge of an equivalence partition or at the smallest incremental distance on either side of an edge, for example the minimum or maximum value of a range.

boundary value analysis: A black-box test design technique, in which test cases are designed based on boundary values.

boundary value coverage: The percentage of boundary values that have been exercised by a test suite.

branch: A basic block that can be selected for execution, based on a program construct in which one of two or more alternative program paths is available, e.g. case, jump, go to, if-then-else.

business process-based testing: An approach to testing in which test cases are designed based on descriptions and/or knowledge of business processes.

capture/playback/replay tool: A type of test execution tool where inputs are recorded during manual testing in order to generate automated test scripts that can be executed later (i.e. replayed). These tools are often used to support automated regression testing.

CAST: Acronym for Computer Aided Software Testing.

cause-effect graph: A graphical representation of inputs and/or stimuli (causes) with their associated outputs (effects), which can be used to design test cases.

cause-effect graphing: A black-box test design technique in which test cases are designed from cause-effect graphs.

changeability: The capability of the software product to enable specified modifications to be implemented.

component: A minimal software item that can be tested in isolation.

component integration testing: Testing performed to expose defects in the interfaces and interaction between integrated components.

component specification: A description of a component's function in terms of its output values for specified input values under specified conditions, and required non-functional behavior (e.g. resource-utilization).

component testing: The testing of individual software components.

concurrency testing: Testing to determine how the occurrence of two or more activities within the same interval of time, achieved either by interleaving the activities or by simultaneous execution, is handled by the component or system.

condition: A logical expression that can be evaluated as True or False, e.g. A>B. See also *test condition*.

condition coverage: The percentage of condition outcomes that have been exercised by a test suite. 100% condition coverage requires each single condition in every decision statement to be tested as True and False.

condition determination coverage: The percentage of all single condition outcomes that independently affect a decision outcome that have been exercised by a test case suite. 100% condition determination coverage implies 100% decision condition coverage.

condition determination testing: A white-box test design technique in which test cases are designed to execute single condition outcomes that independently affect a decision outcome.

condition outcome: The evaluation of a condition to True or False.

condition testing: A white-box test design technique in which test cases are designed to execute condition outcomes.

cost of quality: The total costs incurred on quality activities and issues, and often split into prevention costs, appraisal costs, internal failure costs, and external failure costs.

data-driven testing: A scripting technique that stores test input and expected results in a table or spreadsheet, so that a single control script can execute all of the tests in the table. Data driven testing is often used to support the application of test execution tools such as capture/playback tools.

database integrity testing: Testing the methods and processes used to access and manage the data(base), to ensure access methods, processes, and data rules function as expected and that during access to the database, data is not corrupted or unexpectedly deleted, updated, or created.

defect: A flaw in a component or system that can cause the component or system to fail to perform its required function, e.g. an incorrect statement or data definition. A defect, if encountered during execution, may cause a failure of the component or system.

defect-based test design technique: A procedure to derive and/or select test cases targeted at one or more defect categories, with tests being developed from what is known about the specific defect category.

development testing: Formal or informal testing conducted during the implementation of a component or system, usually in the development environment by developers.

domain: The set from which valid input and/or output values can be selected.

dynamic comparison: Comparison of actual and expected results, performed while the software is being executed, for example by a test execution tool.

dynamic testing: Testing that involves the execution of the software of a component or system.

efficiency: The capability of the software product to provide appropriate performance, relative to the amount of resources used under stated conditions.

efficiency testing: The process of testing to determine the efficiency of a software product.

equivalence partition/class: A portion of an input or output domain for which the behavior of a component or system is assumed to be the same, based on the specification.

equivalence-partition coverage: The percentage of equivalence partitions that have been exercised by a test suite.

exhaustive testing: A test approach in which the test suite comprises all combinations of input values and preconditions.

expected result: The behavior predicted by the specification, or another source, of the component or system under specified conditions.

exploratory testing: An informal test design technique where the tester actively controls the design of the tests as those tests are performed and uses information gained while testing to design new and better tests.

fail: A test is deemed to fail if its actual result does not match its expected result.

failure: Deviation of the component or system from its expected delivery, service, or result.

failure rate: The ratio of the number of failures of a given category to a given unit of measure, e.g. failures per unit of time, failures per number of transactions, failures per number of computer runs.

functional testing: Testing based on an analysis of the specification of the functionality of a component or system.

functionality testing: The process of testing to determine the functionality of a software product.

keyword-driven testing: A scripting technique that uses data files to contain not only test data and expected results, but also keywords related to the application being tested. The keywords are interpreted by special supporting scripts that are called by the control script for the test.

latency (client): Client latency is the time that it takes for a request to reach a server and for the response to travel back (from server to client). Includes network latency and server latency.

latency (network): Network latency is the additional time that it takes for a request (from a client) and a response (from a server) to cross a network until it reaches the intended destination.

latency (server): Server latency is the time the server takes to complete the execution of a request normally made by a client machine.

load profile: A specification of the activity that a component or system being tested may experience in production. A load profile consists of a designated number of virtual users who process a defined set of transactions in a specified time period and according to a predefined operational profile.

load testing: A type of performance testing conducted to evaluate the behavior of a component or system with increasing load, e.g. numbers of parallel users and/or numbers of transactions, to determine what load can be handled by the component or system.

master test plan: A test plan that typically addresses multiple test levels.

metrics: Metrics are the actual measurements obtained by running performance tests. These performance tests include system-related metrics such as CPU, memory, disk I/O, network I/O, and resource utilization levels. The performance tests also include application-specific metrics such as performance counters and timing data.

monitoring tool: A software tool or hardware device that runs concurrently with the component or system under test and supervises, records and/or analyzes the behavior of the component or system.

pass: A test is deemed to pass if its actual result matches its expected result.

pass/fail criteria: Decision rules used to determine whether a test item (function) or feature has passed or failed a test.

performance: The degree to which a system or component accomplishes its designated functions within given constraints regarding processing time and throughput rate.

performance indicator: A high-level metric of effectiveness and/or efficiency used to guide and control progressive development, e.g. lead-time slip for software development.

performance profiling: Definition of user profiles in performance, load and/or stress testing. Profiles should reflect anticipated or actual usage based on an operational profile of a component or system, and hence the expected workload.

performance budgets: Performance budgets are your constraints. Performance budgets specify the amount of resources that you can use for specific scenarios and operations and still be successful.

performance testing: The process of testing to determine the performance of a software product.

performance testing tool: A tool to support performance testing and that usually has two main facilities: load generation and test transaction measurement. Load generation can simulate either multiple users or high volumes of input data. During execution, response time measurements are taken from selected transactions and these are logged. Performance testing tools normally provide reports based on test logs and graphs of load against response times.

record/playback tool: See capture/playback tool.

recorder/scribe: The person who records each defect that is mentioned and any suggestions for process improvement during a review meeting, on a logging form. The recorder/scribe has to ensure that the logging form is readable and understandable.

regression testing: Testing of a previously tested program following modification to ensure that defects have not been introduced or uncovered in unchanged areas of the software, as a result of the changes made. It is performed when the software or its environment is changed.

stress testing: A type of performance testing conducted to evaluate a system or component at or beyond the limits of its anticipated or specified work loads, or with reduced availability of resources such as access to memory or servers.

stress testing tool: A tool that supports stress testing.

test: A set of one or more test cases.

test approach: The implementation of the test strategy for a specific project. It typically includes the decisions made that follow based on the (test) project's goal and the risk assessment carried out, starting points regarding the test process, the test design techniques to be applied, exit criteria, and test types to be performed.

test automation: The use of software to perform or support test activities, e.g. test management, test design, test execution, and results checking.

test case: A set of input values, execution preconditions, expected results, and execution post conditions, developed for a particular objective or test condition, such as to exercise a particular program path or to verify compliance with a specific requirement.

test case design technique: Procedure used to derive and/or select test cases.

test case specification: A document specifying a set of test cases (objective, inputs, test actions, expected results, and execution preconditions) for a test item.

test condition: An item or event of a component or system that could be verified by one or more test cases, e.g. a function, transaction, feature, quality attribute, or structural element.

test cycle: Execution of the test process against a single identifiable release of the test object.

test data: Data that exists (for example, in a database) before a test is executed, and that affects or is affected by the component or system under test.

test data preparation tool: A type of test tool that enables data to be selected from existing databases or created, generated, manipulated, and edited for use in testing.

test design: (1) See *test design specification*. (2) The process of transforming general testing objectives into tangible test conditions and test cases.

test design specification: A document specifying the test conditions (coverage items) for a test item, the detailed test approach, and identifying the associated high-level test cases. [After IEEE 829]

test environment: An environment containing hardware, instrumentation, simulators, software tools, and other support elements needed to conduct a test.

test execution: The process of running a test on the component or system under test, producing actual result(s).

test execution automation: The use of software, e.g. capture/playback tools, to control the execution of tests, the comparison of actual results to expected results, the setting up of test preconditions, and other test control and reporting functions.

test execution tool: A type of test tool that is able to execute other software using an automated test script, e.g. capture/playback.

test generator: See *test data preparation tool*.

test harness: A test environment comprising stubs and drivers needed to execute a test.

test plan: A document describing the scope, approach, resources, and schedule of intended test activities. It identifies amongst others test items, the features to be tested, the testing tasks, who will do each task, the degree of tester independence, the test environment, the test design techniques, entry and exit criteria to be used, and the rationale for their choice, and any risks requiring contingency planning. It is a record of the test planning process.

test run: Execution of a test on a specific version of the test object.

test script: Commonly used to refer to a test procedure specification, especially an automated one.

test set: See test suite

test suite: A set of several test cases for a component or system under test, where the post condition of one test is often used as the precondition for the next one.

tester: A skilled professional who is involved in the testing of a component or system.

testing: The process consisting of all life-cycle activities, both static and dynamic, concerned with planning, preparation, and evaluation of software products and related work products to determine that they satisfy specified requirements, to demonstrate that they are fit for purpose, and to detect defects.

time behavior: See *performance.*

volume testing: Testing where the system is subjected to large volumes of data.

For more terms, visit: http://www.istqb.org/downloads/glossary-1.0.pdf.

Index

Proxy Server configuration element, configuring 61
test cases, recording 81, 82
test plan, creating 63-65
timers, adding 65
UDV, adding 82, 83
JMeter requirements
JVM 21
JVM
about 21
JVM, requirements
JMeter plug-ins, building 22
Java complier used 22
JMeter stable version 1.8, downloading 22
JSSE, downloading 21

L

listeners
about 35
Aggregate Graph listener control panel 35
features 36
load testing
about 51
preparing for 52
test cases, determining 53
load testing, preparing for
important expectations 52
tips 52, 53
logic controllers
about 34
loop controller control panel 34

M

manual testing vs automate testing 11

P

performance testing
about 51
load testing 51
post-processor elements 42
pre-processor elements 41

R

regular expression
about 93
control panel 95
pattern, verifying 96
using 94
return on investment. *See* **ROI**
ROI 12

S

samplers 32
samplers, controllers
HTTP Request sampler control panel 32

T

testing, FTP server
Gold FTP server 99
multiple requests, demonstrating 99
requirements 99
threadNum function, appending 100
test Plan
about 27
elements 27, 29
test plan
about 18
building 42
control panel 28, 29
enhancing 87
running 47, 84, 85
saving 47
web test plan, building 88
test plan, JMeter
results, interpreting 68-70
running 68
test plan, running
column headings 48
test plan, thread group
elements 18
thread group
about 29
control panel 30, 31
timers
about 37
constant timer control panel 38

U

W

Thank you for buying
Apache JMeter

Packt Open Source Project Royalties

When we sell a book written on an Open Source project, we pay a royalty directly to that project. Therefore by purchasing Scalix, Packt will have given some of the money received to the Apache Jkarta Project.

In the long term, we see ourselves and you — customers and readers of our books — as part of the Open Source ecosystem, providing sustainable revenue for the projects we publish on. Our aim at Packt is to establish publishing royalties as an essential part of the service and support a business model that sustains Open Source.

If you're working with an Open Source project that you would like us to publish on, and subsequently pay royalties to, please get in touch with us.

Writing for Packt

We welcome all inquiries from people who are interested in authoring. Book proposals should be sent to authors@packtpub.com. If your book idea is still at an early stage and you would like to discuss it first before writing a formal book proposal, contact us; one of our commissioning editors will get in touch with you.

We're not just looking for published authors; if you have strong technical skills but no writing experience, our experienced editors can help you develop a writing career, or simply get some additional reward for your expertise.

About Packt Publishing

Packt, pronounced 'packed', published its first book "Mastering phpMyAdmin for Effective MySQL Management" in April 2004 and subsequently continued to specialize in publishing highly focused books on specific technologies and solutions.

Our books and publications share the experiences of your fellow IT professionals in adapting and customizing today's systems, applications, and frameworks. Our solution-based books give you the knowledge and power to customize the software and technologies you're using to get the job done. Packt books are more specific and less general than the IT books you have seen in the past. Our unique business model allows us to bring you more focused information, giving you more of what you need to know, and less of what you don't.

Packt is a modern, yet unique publishing company, which focuses on producing quality, cutting-edge books for communities of developers, administrators, and newbies alike. For more information, please visit our website: www.PacktPub.com.

Quickstart Apache Axis2

ISBN: 978-1-847192-86-8   Paperback: 168 pages

A practical guide to creating quality web services

1. Complete practical guide to Apache Axis 2

2. Using Apache Axis2 to create secure, reliable web services quickly

3. Write Axis2 modules to enhance web services' security, reliability, robustness and transaction support

Tapestry 5

ISBN: 978-1-847193-07-0   Paperback: 280 pages

A step-by-step guide to Java Web development with the developer-friendly Apache Tapestry framework

1. Latest version of Tapestry web development framework

2. Get working with Tapestry components

3. Gain hands-on experience developing an example site

4. Practical step-by-step tutorial

Please check **www.PacktPub.com** for information on our titles

6795137R00079

Printed in Great Britain
by Amazon.co.uk, Ltd.,
Marston Gate.